Breath of My Ancestors

Reflections from the Conscience of an African in America

Breath of My Ancestors

Reflections From the Conscience of an African in America

http://livinglegacy.ning.com/profile/TyGrayEL

Published in the United States by BOMA
ISBN: **978-0-615-36188-8**
Library of Congress Cataloging-in-Publication data pending
10 9 8 76 5 4 3 2 1

Breath of My Ancestors

Reflections from the Conscience of an African in America

Ty Gray-EL

Contents

Introduction 13

Africa My Africa 15

Opinion on Hurricanes 16

Breath of My Ancestors 18

Nawlin's Home 21

Know Yourself 23

My Mother Said 24

Commentary on Prejudice (The Cream Shall Rise) 26

The Cream Shall Rise 31

Grandma's Eyes 35

Wake Up Sleeping Giants 36

Commentary on Addiction & Sleeping Giants 38

Heroin's Song 43

Blown Away 45

Life in a Pipe 46

Commentary on America's Drug Problem 48

Little Shop of Sorrow 50

Ode/Owed To Reneé	51
Domestic Acceptance (Forgotten September)	53
Commentary on Anger	55
Appeal to an Angry Man	61
Root Out Murder – Put Guns Aside	63
How Can You Sleep	64
Seriously, How Can You Sleep	65
Commentary on Conservative Right	70
What If Reparations	78
From Caint See to Caint See	81
Commentary on the Confederate	85
We Must Never Forget	90
Deferred Dreams	93
In Spite Of	95
North Wind	97
Liberty Miss Liberty	99
Commentary on 18 Missing Years	101
18 Years	112

Commentary on Over There
Life after Death & Judgment Day 114

Over There 116

Judgment Day 117

The Devil Left This Evening 119

Church Search 121

One Man 123

Commentary on Death by Decision 125

Death By Decision 127

Commentary on Anthrax 128

Anthrax Blues (Postal Workers Nightmare) 129

"9/11 Kamikaze" 130

Winged Hatred 131

Future Doubt 132

Ain't You Tired 133

Teach Them 135

Labels 137

The Keys 139

Bless the Day (Where Would You Be Without Us) 141

Appreciation for Granville T. Woods 144

Breath of My Ancestors

Calling All Rappers 146

Respect the Flow (OG Rapper's Prayer) 148

My Pain Rose 150

Trapped 152

What Happened to the Passion? 154

Where In the World Is Negro? 156

"Negrosity" 158

When 160

My 40 Acres & My Mule 161

Commentary on Muhammad Ali 162

Thank You Muhammad Ali 164

Where I Came From 166

Where Were You Dad? (A Penitentiary Saga) 168

One Degree of Separation 171

Opportunity 172

Anatomy of the 7 174

12 Rounds to Victory 176

A Wedding Prayer 177

Marriage Instructions 178

Big Chair Chess Club 179

Cloud Song 180

Heal a Parent–Heal a Child 182

History of the Ad 183

Plump 185

Wanted 186

Melanin, Sweet Melanin 187

Sole/Soul Sista 189

Opinion on: Stress 191

Stress Test 196

Slam Your Stress 197

Valley of Despair 198

The Flood 199

The Test 201

Thanks Oprah 202

You Special 203

Redeem the Dream 204

Your True Worth 206

Seven Little Boys 207

Sirens & Police Badges 208

Watch 209

The Mighty Pen 211

Aging 213

Remember Me 214

Voices of Civil Rights 215

When I Think of Malcolm 217

Colonel J W Alford 221

Ignatious Holloway 225

Bathsheba Hempstead 228

Ebenezer Carter 231

Paco Suarez Hope 232

Cyrus James 237

Amos Sweeney 238

Ethel Ann Hardison 241

Thaddeus Whitmore 243

Hannibal Haskins 244

The Lynching of Sam Hose…Author Unknown 245

A Black Woman's Smile 247

EPILOGUE 250

First, I give all honor, adoration, thanksgiving and praise to my Creator and honor to my ancestors upon whose shoulders I stand today.

By the grace of almighty God this book is dedicated
to the indomitable spirit and breath of my ancestors. It is a tribute to the African/Edenic people who triumphed over the most unspeakable holocaust in the history of mankind, chattel slavery. This is a testimony to the people who, in spite of being subjected to every conceivable method of mental and physical terrorism, still rise. It is a treatise written to shed light on the fact that Africa is not the 'dark continent' as many would have you believe. On the contrary, all the arts and sciences of the civilized world originated from the genius of the melanised people of the world beginning in Africa. It is an effort to dispel the myths and prove false the lies that have been told about the historical contributions of my people so we may take back the legacy of the African identities of Imhotep, Jesus, Moses, Abraham, David, Solomon, Aesop, Lilith, Mary, Ruth, Cleopatra and countless others that were stolen. This book is in fact a prayer that we relearn how to love ourselves so much that we can find neither the time nor the inclination to hate others.

-Ty Gray-EL

INTRODUCTION

This treatise is not to offend, but to question. It is not to blame, but to illustrate. It is written with the understanding that love is the only savior of humanity and out of respect for love it has been penned. Love is the strongest element that the Universe reveals to us and it is our duty to find a way to immerse ourselves in its omnipotent power.

My ultimate goal in writing this book is to petition, appeal and plead with so-called African-American black men and women, as well as those scattered throughout the Diaspora, to love yourselves. That's it! No more, no less, just love yourself.

Therefore, I challenge you to open your mind to the possibilities of love and start with yourself. If you start with yourself, the rest will take care of itself. If *you* start loving *You* unconditionally, you will save the world one individual at a time. The whole world is seeking peace and the only way it can be obtained is through love. Love is such a fine ideal that even poets, philosophers and greatest thinkers are hard pressed unearthing words to define it.

When we think of love we think of it as an emotion which includes affection, friendship, kinship, kindness, tenderness, sympathy, empathy, benevolence, good feelings, fondness, devotion, care and passion. All of these are attributes of love and come as close to a description as we can get with our finite minds.

My request of you, dear reader, is that you consciously make an effort from this day forward to apply these attributes to yourself as a code of conduct. If you actively apply these characteristics to yourself, the natural progression of your application will automatically trigger a spill-over effect and like air, LOVE will permeate everywhere. Then, our ancestors will not have suffered and died in vain.

"Love is the only force capable of transforming an enemy into a friend."

-Dr. Martin Luther King Jr.

"Tell them that the sacrifice was not in vain. Tell them that by habits of thrift and economy, by way of the industrial school and college, we are coming. We are crawling up, working up, bursting up: Coming through oppression, unjust discrimination and prejudice. But throughout them all, we are coming up, and with proper habits, intelligence and property, there is no power on earth that can permanently stay our progress."

-Booker T. Washington,
Up from Slavery

Africa My Africa...

Drum beats herald civilization's dawning…
Cradle land of the initiate…
Mother of infinite wisdom…
Conquering hordes have trampled on your bosom
unappreciative of your ancient splendor…
Immeasurable treasures buried in your bowels…
Mined by foreign invaders with careless laxatives…
Warm and fertile womb of creation…
You gave birth to immortal souls…
Distorted by pagan influences…
Africa, sweet Africa…
Raped and pillaged, plundered and plowed
by infidels with no respect…
You cry and oil tears drip down
your blood stained mountains…
You perspire and diamonds rise from your pores…
Africa, my Africa…
You bleed the blood of the blessed chosen…
Your veins spew crimson rain down
on the heads of the unjust…
And unlike Pontius Pilot, they cannot
wash their hands…
Africa, my dear sweet Africa…
You shall be vindicated…
Black pearls will one day emerge
from the shells of capitalistic indifference…
And you shall, Phoenix-like, soar
above the forest of all…
Mother of us all…
You gave birth to the King and Queen of civilization…
And you shall have your due…
My Africa, sweet Africa…

Opinion on Hurricanes

According to meteorologists, astronomers, archeologists, seismologists and virtually every other kind of "ologist" that study weather patterns and catastrophic weather conditions, the "hurricane" is absolutely the most forceful set of weather circumstances known to man. Sebastian Junger author of *The Perfect Storm*, comments on such weather by stating "a mature hurricane is by far the most powerful event on earth." He also said, "The combined nuclear arsenals of the United States and the former Soviet Union do not contain enough energy to keep a hurricane going for one day." There have been reports of hurricane whirlpools stretching more than 2000 miles wide with 75 to 100 foot high waves that have sustained wind speeds of more than 200 miles per hour, lasting 7 consecutive days and more. Storm trackers say these phenomena seem to have a life of their own. They can turn around mid-fury and go in the opposite direction or veer to the left or right as if a spirit were moving them.

The fact is we are all spirit from the everlasting past unto the never-ending days to come. Humans are the breath made flesh and so our very essence, that which we cannot see, is spirit. The Bible says in Luke 8:24 that when Jesus rebuked the wind and raging waters the storm subsided. The people were shocked that he could talk to the elements and they would obey. It is further reported in the *Essene Chronicles* and the *Aquarian Gospel* that on that same occasion, Jesus told his Disciples that they had identical power and that they should not marvel at what he did.

He cautioned people at every turn not to worship him, but to praise God. He said that we all have the capacity to do what he did. *Aquarian Gospel* says in Chap.117:33-36 "And Jesus stood; he raised his hand;

he talked unto the spirits of the winds and waves as men would talk with men. And, lo, the winds blew not; the waves came tremblingly and kissed his feet; the sea was calm." And then he said, "You men of little faith, where is your faith? For you can speak and winds and waves will hear and will obey." The disciples were amazed. They said, "Who is this man that even winds and waves obey his voice?"

So I pose a question; if our spirit has the power to talk to the elements to make them obey and stop, then would it not stand to reason that those same elements would obey and start? Remember we are the breath made flesh and what is air but breath and what is wind but breath?

Consider that hurricanes seldom if ever come off the Pacific, the Arctic or the Indian Oceans. Hurricanes originate in the Atlantic Ocean. They all get started around the western shores of Africa, take virtually the same route as the slave trade and slam primarily into the southern states of America. They seem to have a mind of their own, turn around mid-fury and take whichever direction they choose.

Meteorologists stated that at one point the massive cloud cover of hurricane Frances was as large as the state of Texas and that 119 separate tornadoes spun off hurricane Ivan alone. We all saw hurricanes Charlie, Frances and Ivan during the summer of 2004 cause massive damage and in 2005 hurricane Katrina wreaked havoc and epic destruction. For all the above reasons and many more, I submit that hurricanes are the BREATH OF MY ANCESTORS.

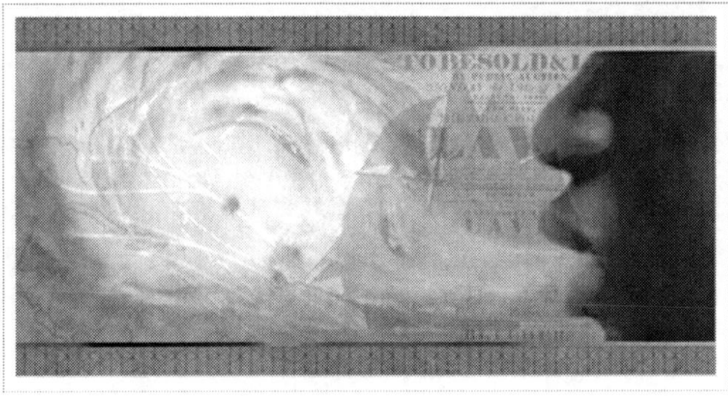

Breath of My Ancestors

(The Hurricane)

There's a truth that must be told
Its force can't be contained
about the history
and the mystery
in the rage of hurricanes

For you must know the reasons
why gale force winds do blow
and disburse their vicious vengeance
on southern states below

You see, the bodies of my people
through the Middle Passage came
as cargo in slave ships
so a beast could lay quitclaim

And their limbs were battered and broken
by a heathen with no shame
who stole us from our homes
then promptly changed our names

But now the laws of cause and effect
so appropriately germane
come collecting unpaid taxes
in the form of hurricanes

You thought our spirits were beaten
you thought our spirits were tamed
but instead of us defeatin'
God's temper you inflamed
Now retribution comes to visit
on the winds of hurricanes
Storm clouds gather over Africa
full of slavery's suffering and pain

They marshal their momentum
full of vengeful hard black rain
dead-set upon America
as if possessed, insane

And since all those cries for mercy
fell on deaf ears in vain
you must feel the wrath
and the fury of hurricanes

For the girls you stole from Senegal
and the boys from Ivory Coast
the spirit of those ancestors
haunt Louisianans most

Cause of all the slave-ship harbors
in the many ports of call
yours were the most insidious
the vilest of them all

And for all you island dwellers
to whom this verse pertains
your shores made shelter for sellers
of human beings in chains

Thus, the breath of my ancestors
forge a spiritual weather vane
that plots a course of sorrow
via the gale of hurricanes

In cargo holds
you laid 20 million souls
like spoons in kitchen cabinets
But now the winds blow down
entire towns
leaving tents to pitch and maggots

And the law of just requital
extracting its just due
says you must pay
for the games you play
Florida and Mississippi too

So, if the next gale wind you hear
evokes real fear
and the terror seems inhumane
It's Just…It's Just
It's just the Breath of My Ancestors
in the spirit of the hurricane…

Nawlin's Home

Swing Low sweet chariot-comin' for to carry me home
Swing Low sweet chariot-comin' for to carry me home
HOME
Seven whole feet below sea level…
Chief export, intoxication…
Chief import, the intoxicated…
Decadence bought and sold on Bourbon and Beaker
Streets while trumpets blow…
Nawlin's-where the dead never go into the ground…
Where restless souls sing the Ninth Ward Blues…
Swing Low…
8-29-05 Katrina comes to call with revenge in mind…
Ancestral gust of winds and torrential rains blow the
covers of the callous, exposing the slimy, sleazy
underbelly of America's Dictators…
Citizens converted instantaneously into refugees
by government decree…
With Bush-isms like, "Families is where our nation finds
hope, where wings take dream…and
"You're doing a great job Brownie!"
Forced to see my family separated just like that 1863
Canal Street auction block…
Forced to hear muffled, gurgling, forlorn cries of me
drowning in my own living room…
Forced to feel like if my skin was different
they'd be here already…
Forced to taste the putrid, gagging vapors
rising from garbage and fecal matter…
Forced to smell fear rising from my own pours as I wait
for death on my flag-draped rooftop…
Muddy waters agitated by 140 mile an hour
deep breaths influenced by agony…
The agony of totin' that barge, liftin' that bale, gettin'
a little drunk and landin' in jail…
Muddy waters moved by unrelenting gale-force winds
that took the Super out of the Dome and replaced it
with hopeless muddied aspirations…

Home of the blues where the scent of Magnolia corrupts
my sense of smell, distorts my nostrils…
…appears to be sweet, but *is* the sweat of oppression
dripping from the last 300 years…
Nawlin's, which still, to this day, holds the record for
auctioning off more slaves than any other place
in human history…
Home of Pirate's Alley where gangster bandits forced
slaves to walk the plank at sword-point…
Home of the French Quarter where Maroons, Octoroons,
Creoles and Mulattoes were made…
Home where the French quartered and bogged us down
for being Maroons, Octoroons, Creoles and Mulattoes...
Swing Low…sweet chariot, please come
and take me home…
Wish you would carry me home cause this one
ain't treatin' me right…
Damned if this Houston Astrodome don't remind me
of those Pic-Nics in Lynchburg…
Picked us then, the same as now…picked my uncle to go
to Kentucky; picked my son to go to Georgia…
this ain't no Pic-Nic, or is it?

Know Yourself

Weak as you are bronze child of the dust
Humble, as you ought to be
If you'd raise your thoughts a notch above lust
what infinite wisdom you'd see

Fearfully and wonderfully are you made
adulation should be given your Maker
with constant reverence steadily displayed
from the cradle to the undertaker

Why of all creatures can you alone stand
erect, walking straight with head raised
No other entity can make demands
your Designer should forever be praised

Why is consciousness bestowed on you alone
and when exactly did it arrive
Your flesh certainly cannot condone
and your bones alone can't contrive

Something is added to you my friend
unlike to what you see
a special ingredient blended in
you'd best treat it reverently

Flesh doesn't think, bones won't reason
blood cannot understand
You'd best take pride
in your Spirit inside
and let the God in you command

Know yourself…

My Mother Said

My mother said she was African
no matter where she stood
you could take her feet off African soil
but you couldn't take her African good

My mother said her mother
was the mother of civilization
you could take her name
you could cause her shame
but you couldn't take that salutation

My mother said I was royalty
crowned Prince of the Motherland
she said I was the one
God's promised son
and back home I was truly grand

My mother said my melanin
was a gift and I should be proud
she said darkness of hue
is God's gift to you
your personal protective shroud

My mother said my hair
like Sampson's represented strength
She said one shouldn't hide
their race pride
the power's in the lock not the length

My mother said many things
and most I put on a shelf
but one thing is clear, I can still hear
"SON, LEARN TO LOVE YOUR SELF"

She said Jesus was African, Noah was African
Moses was African, looked nothing like
Charlton Heston.
She said everybody from the Islands came from Africa,
Jamaicans-Africans, Haitians-Africans,
Cubans-Africans
King David, African,
Solomon wisest of all kings, African.
She said everybody on this planet
came from Africa, originally

My mother said many things
and most I put on a shelf
but one thing is clear, I can still hear
"SON, LEARN TO LOVE YOUR SELF"

*"It is a peculiar sensation, this double consciousness,
this sense of always
looking at one's self through the eyes of
others. . . . One ever feels his twoness,—
an American, a Negro; two souls, two
thoughts, two unreconciled strivings; two
warring ideals in one dark body, whose
dogged strength alone keeps it from being
torn asunder."*

— W. E. B. Du Bois, *The Souls of
Black Folk* (1903)

Commentary on Prejudice - The Cream Shall Rise

One thing that saddens me deeply in the year 2010 is that we still have people who honestly believe that Africa is the "Dark Continent." This phrase being loosely used to describe a people who are backward, slow and contributed very little to civilization. Most of the literature available to African American youth today, especially in public schools and the majority of private schools depict our history as beginning with the slave trade. Very few positive historical facts are taught to black people of the African Diaspora inhabiting North America at this time.

It is alleged that the greatest thinkers of all time are all of European descent, like Ptolemy, Plato and Socrates. We are taught that Aristotle wrote more than 1000 books (which was proven to be a chronological impossibility) as is pointed out in "Stolen Legacy" by George G.M. James.(1954) We are instructed that virtually every worthwhile achievement, philosophically, scientifically, scholastically and historically are a result of great minds developed and shaped in Europe. Yet, the actual truth is that every one of these so-called Greek philosophers received their information and training either directly or indirectly from the "Cradle-Land of the Initiate" in Egypt (Kemet), which is still an African country despite efforts to change its geography.

We have been taught that Hippocrates (460-380? BC) is the father of medicine, when in fact, noted historian and author of several volumes on African history, Professor John Henrik Clarke proves that Imhotep (2650-2580 BC) practiced medicine in Africa two thousand-two hundred years before Hippocrates was even born. Furthermore, Sir William Osler, author of the book *Evolution of Modern Medicine* refers to Imhotep as "the first physician to stand out clearly from the mists of antiquity." Professor Clarke added that the Temple of Imhotep was mankind's first hospital. He wrote: "Egyptian physicians were frequently specialists. Some were dentists; others were occultists, surgeons and specialists in diseases of the stomach, and so on. In the course of their work, they made many discoveries of lasting value."

Edward McNall Burns and Philip Lee Ralph point out that Egyptians discovered the value of catharsis and characterized the curative properties of many modern drugs. They compiled the first "Materia Medica" or "Catalogue of Medicines". Many of their medicines, both scientific and mystical, were carried into Europe by the Greeks and are still used today.

What I honestly do not understand is why a people would go to such great lengths to hide the admirable works of another people? If all people are created equal and endowed by their creator, then the accomplishments of all humans should be a source of pride to all humans. Why would a race of people steal the legacy of another people? If I am proud of my heritage and love myself, why would I take the identity of another? And why would Europeans, like Alexander, go to such great lengths as to destroy and deface ancient artifacts depicting our magnificent ancestor's facial features?

Also, what is it that makes people of European extract take advantage of every opportunity they can to exploit people of the African Diaspora? Why is racism so ingrained in the psyche of Europeans? Why do whites feel the need to colonize the world and make everyone slaves, consciously enslaving every non-European race they encounter?

And finally, when will we come to grips with and acknowledge the following facts? Africans were the first civilized people of the world. Africa is not the "Dark

Continent," but in fact, the light and knowledge of all the world's great civilizations came from its womb?

Here is an example that highlights the deception and deliberate lies spread by racism and white supremacy. . For the most part, the continent of Africa is depicted as a jungle or forest with a bunch of spear-chucking, bare-naked bushmen running around foraging for food. The true fact is that even though Africa has far more landmass than America, the United States has more wild forest per square mile than Africa does. America is comprised of about 38 percent forestland, while only 28 percent of Africa is actually forest covered. Africa has always been made up of both large and small cities with thriving civilized metropolitan areas dating back thousands of years. Yet, the images we are continually fed are of loin-cloth-wearing savages with bones in their noses and plates in their lips being rescued by the white Bwana, Tarzan.

The truth is quite the contrary. We have a glorious and illustrious history and have left a wonderful legacy to the world. We must find ways to obtain this information, distribute it among ourselves, learn to love our true history and appreciate our magnificent and myriad contributions to this planet. We need to take ownership, responsibility and stewardship of what is rightfully ours. In other words we need to re-cognize to de-colonize our minds and seize back control of the truth of Our-Story rejecting His-Story.

When I was seven years old, my grandmother taught me one of the greatest lessons I've ever learned. In the early 60's the milkman would deliver milk to houses in glass quart bottles. He would wear a white hat, a white uniform, wore white shoes and drove a white milk truck. He'd always deliver early in the morning, usually before most people got up. This one spring morning, she told me to bring the milk in and made me sit down and look closely at the bottle. She asked me what I saw. I said, "I see milk Grandma, that's all I see." She made me sit there and stare at that bottle of milk more than five minutes.

Again she asked, "What do you see?" Now as you might imagine, I'm a (forced to sit) frustrated little seven year- old kid who thinks his Grandmother is trippin' because all I see is the milk in the bottle. She tells me that I cannot leave my seat until I describe what I see, and to keep looking closely. So I'm there twitching and fidgeting when it dawns on me that there is a quarter inch line at the top that's darker than the milk at the bottom. She nodded, pleased, saying "that's right son, that's cream on top of the milk."

So I asked her what cream was and she explained that the cream was the essence, the sweetest, thickest and most nutritious part of the milk. This was before we became accustomed to this distilled homogenized milk being sold today, Then she shook the bottle forcefully, set it back in front of me and asked me again what I saw. I noticed immediately that the line was gone and all the milk looked the same.

I said, "That was a neat trick Grandma." She smiled and told me to sit there and keep looking. I must have sat there another full five minutes gazing at that bottle. I squirmed as I fought to keep my attention on the milk. Then it hit me, like a smack on the forehead, the line was back. At some point while I wasn't looking the cream had risen back to the top of that bottle. I shouted, "Grandma, its back, the cream is back on top! How did you do that?" She smiled and said she didn't do it, God did it, nature did it. She said: "The cream is the essence and the best part of the milk and it always rises to the top." She said, "You, my son, are the cream of humanity. All humanity started with your ancestors in Africa and don't you ever forget it. You are neither a "nigger" nor a "Negro"; you are a Race Man and descendant of Kings and Queens. You are royalty and the cream of this planet and just like that cream rose to the top of that milk bottle, you will one day rise back to the top of civilization, because the cream shall always rise."

That lesson prompted me to write, years later, in loving memory of my dearest, wonderful grandmother, Thelma (Miss Polly) Johnson: "The Cream Shall Rise."

The Cream Shall Rise

Listen Africans Diaspora
and you shall be told
of your glorious history
in the days of old
When you were Kings and Queens
of commerce and trade
when the tubs you bathed in
were gold in-laid
When your bodies were covered
with the finest silk
and you drank from silver goblets
the sweetest milk
When your bedposts were made of oak
and the finest cedar
and the world sought advice
from the African Leader
Yes, listen dear children
and you shall hear
how you sailed the seven seas
without any fear
How you gave the world medicine
and cured those ill
and constructed awesome Pyramids
with your mighty will
How when some of the world's people
were living in caves
your cities had streetlights
and the roads were paved
Why, when some were scared of fire
and thought the world was flat
you had smoke coming from chimneys
and globes on floor mats
How we wore the finest rubies
diamonds and pearls
and filled the universities
with our boys and girls

How we introduced writing
so mankind could read
and concerning arts and science
Africans took the lead
Yes, listen my people
and you shall know
how you gave the world
splendor a few decades ago
How you built the Sphinx
how you swam the Nile
then sailed up and down it
to relax for a while
How you marched through storms and war
defending God's name
then wrote laws of anatomy
to contemplate your frame
How you were the first people
to develop speech
then you created the Griot
so you could learn and teach
Yes, listen good people
check your history, recall
you carried the torch
that lit the way for us all
And try to remember
as you go through life's maze
that one of these good old glorious days
You'll be back on top
for the cream shall rise
Just as sure as the sun lights the eastern skies

THE CREAM SHALL RISE!

"The significance of African history is shown, though not overtly, in the very effort to deny anything worthy of the name of history to Africa and the African peoples. This widespread, and well nigh successful endeavor, maintained through some five centuries, to erase African history from the general record, is a fact which of itself should be quite conclusive to thinking and open minds. For it is logical and apparent that no such undertaking would ever have been carried on, and at such length, in order to obscure and to bury what is actually of little or no significance."

-John Henrik Clarke, *Worlds Great Men of Color* (1972)

"Those piles of ruins which you see in that narrow valley watered by the Nile, are the remains of opulent cities, the pride of the ancient kingdom of Ethiopia. ... There a people, now forgotten, discovered while others were yet barbarians, the elements of the arts and sciences. A race of men now rejected from society for their sable skin and frizzled hair, founded on the study of the laws of nature, those civil and religious systems which still govern the universe." - Count Constantin Francois de Volney, *Voyage en Egypte 1787*

Grandma's Eyes

Grandma's eyes twinkled like city lights
Gleaming with a secret smile
Looking back over centuries, looking forward
past tomorrow
Grandma's eyes spoke, they said
"It's gonna be alright child."
Grandma's eyes saw the other side, they'd cross over
Sometimes I could see her seeing…she just knew
Grandma's eyes could heal and nip and tuck and sew
with laser-like precision
Grandma's eyes could x-ray souls
They whispered, "There is no death!"
Grandma's eyes twinkled like night stars
Illuminating dark alleys
Eliminating dark shadows
Grandma's eyes were blankets in winter
They were a cool breeze in heat
They knew not defeat
They cared
Grandma's eyes had the gift of understanding
They loved!
I loved my Grandma's eyes!

Wake Up Sleeping Giants

People of the African Diaspora
Please heed these few verses
Get up off your deathbed
This whole world's been misled
See, Ham was not subject to curses

Melanised people of the world
A trick has been played on your minds
A scheme so divisive
So incredibly derisive
As to make your own soul undermine

Dark skinned people of the planet
A devilish game has been played
You're not the minority
In fact the majority
Straight victims of a cruel charade

Good people of the African Diaspora
Understand each word that's been said
You're not the worst people
You are the first people
Wake up, you've been misled

Wake up you sleeping Giants
Black, tan, red, yellow and brown
You can rise from your slumber
Put evil asunder
And turn this whole world around

Wake up…! Wakeup…! Wakeup…!

"Bringing the gifts that my ancestors gave
I am the dream and the hope of the slave
I rise
I rise
I rise"

Maya Angelou – "*And Still I Rise*"

Commentary on Addiction & Sleeping Giants

When we talk about "sleeping giants" the most effective method of lulling and keeping blacks asleep is the dispensing of drugs and alcohol into our communities. One of the ways this society perpetuates the "rich get richer and the poor get poorer" syndrome is through the proliferation of drugs inside its poorest neighborhoods. You tell me what's wrong with the following, picture?

When I was 12 years old, I was introduced to heroin. By the time I was 13 I was a full-blown heroin addict. Make no mistake about my attitude concerning this, I'm not bragging. This is not something I'm proud of. It is just a fact. I am here now to take full responsibility for my actions after more than 29 years of sobriety. I know I abused myself, my family and my neighbors and I accept that responsibility. My question is who is going to take responsibility for making all those drugs available in my neighborhood?

You see neither I, nor any of my associates had the wherewithal to manufacture or distribute heroin and cocaine. We certainly weren't chemists who had the capacity to convert the poppies. None of us had access to the laboratories necessary to process the finished product and then make it available to us. So at 13 years old, how did I get addicted in the first place and more importantly, who benefited from my addiction? Where are those profits and where is that money?

The National Clearing House for Alcohol and Drug Information reports that "at least 300 metric tons or 10,500,200 ounces of cocaine are imported into the U.S. each year." We as a people, African-Americans, have little to no importation capabilities yet the majority of that cocaine finds its way to our neighborhoods. How is that possible? Maybe we're just biologically cocaine magnets. Maybe we have heroin heat-seeking devices built into our DNA (Deoxyribonucleic Acid) that attracts it to wherever we are. Maybe it's just a coincidence or perhaps our neighborhoods have a natural proclivity and magnetic density that draws illicit drugs to its street corners.

According to the National Institute of Drug Abuse (NIDA) From 2007 to 2008, the percentage of 10th-graders reporting lifetime, past year, and past month use of **any illicit drug other than marijuana** declined significantly. Lifetime use decreased from 18.2 to 15.9 percent, past-year use declined from 13.1 to 11.3 percent, and past-month use decreased from 6.9 to 5.3 percent.

I only refer to the previous statistics to make the point that if the above is true and the following is also true then the so-called "war on drugs" has always been a fiasco. The actual war has been on our people in inner cities, not on drugs. The White House requested $16 billion for the War on Drugs in the 2008 budget, an increase of $818 million, or 5.4% of the amount allotted in 2007. At the same time the FBI reported the number of arrests for illegal drug use increased.

Evidently somebody's math is off or I'm just dense in the head because it stands to reason that if drug arrests went up then drug usage should have gone down. So why would we need a 5% increase. It would seem to me that we would need to spend less money since there were less people to spend it on. I think they call that "fuzzy math." I never hear any astute politicians asking these kinds of questions. We're steadily auditing Wall Street and probing into Tiger Woods sex life when we should also be double and triple-checking the government agencies that constantly advance their own agendas and never really investigate what actually should be investigated.

We're forever catching nightly news clips of the neighborhood-scapegoat (brother in the hood) who was foolish enough to think he was actually benefiting from selling drugs in his own community. You always see
Storm trooper-like terrorists dressed in police uniforms tearing down some neighborhood crack house door, coming out with a black man on the six o'clock news, usually handcuffed with the headlines proclaiming another victory in the war on drugs. Yet you seldom if ever see the people get arrested who provided them the substances in the first place.

Then the brother is carted off to jail to work for slave labor wages. Most citizens think that the 8 out of 10 black or brown men and women who are incarcerated are just laying around languishing in a jail cell when the real truth is they are working and producing for the State or Federal Government. All this occurs while the real villain cozy's up to yet another neighborhood casualty (soft target) and dupes him in to ruining his life.

I am willing to stake my life that if any real investigative work were ever done on drug distribution the trails would all lead to corporate megalomaniacs, senators, congressmen and many more so-called 'distinguished gentlemen' living lives of leisure in America.

According to the U.S. Department of Justice, "53% of state prison inmates, 74% of county and city jail inmates, and 87% of federal inmates were imprisoned for offenses which involved neither harm, nor the threat of harm to a victim." Victimless crimes are what they're called. In other words, their crimes were *drug related* where they, themselves were the victims. So if black people are the actual victims, who are the actual villains? Where are the real criminals?

Prison populations in 2010 now exceed the combined populations of Wyoming, Alaska and North Dakota. If there are more than two point five million people incarcerated in the U.S. then that is close to one percent of the entire population. Something is wrong with this statistic and why are eight out of ten American inmates of African or Latino descent? Why are black and brown people so disproportionately affected? Why are our neighborhoods so ravaged? Why is there (as of this writing January 2010) not one white child locked up in the District of Columbia's youth detention facilities? One hundred percent of the incarcerated youth in America's capital city are either black or brown, not one white youth. Somebody please explain?

Make no mistake; it is by design and not by happenstance. Why do drug investigations always stop at the middleman? How did Junebug get the dope in the first place and who brought them to him?

I suffered from addiction for 15 years. I started because I thought it was glamorous. I called myself keeping up with the Jones's not knowing I'd end up with a "Jones". I thought all the fly guys in the hood did it and I didn't want to be left out. In reality it was 15 consecutive years of being left out because they represented total non-productivity.

How many more like me were crippled in such a manner all over the country? Hundreds of thousands? Millions? Tens of millions down through the years? How many potential doctors, engineers and entrepreneurs have squandered their genius to the evil of drug addiction, never to recover? And who is it that ultimately gains from such enterprise or in this case, lack of enterprise? These questions never get answered, hell they don't even get asked.

I wrote the following pieces about heroin and cocaine addiction because folk need to know that it is an illness, a sickness, and a disease. They were written so people would consider the mindset of the addicted and think over the cause rather than focus on the effect. It was written also for you to consider that maybe the glory and the shame have been misplaced. The criminal and the victim's role have been reversed and it is a crying shame. It is a real problem and we're viewing it from all the wrong angles. When I suffered from the illness I continuously sang "Heroin's Song." Sometimes I felt like I'd been "Blown Away" and I know that those who find themselves living in one, are sick and tired of "Life In A Pipe."

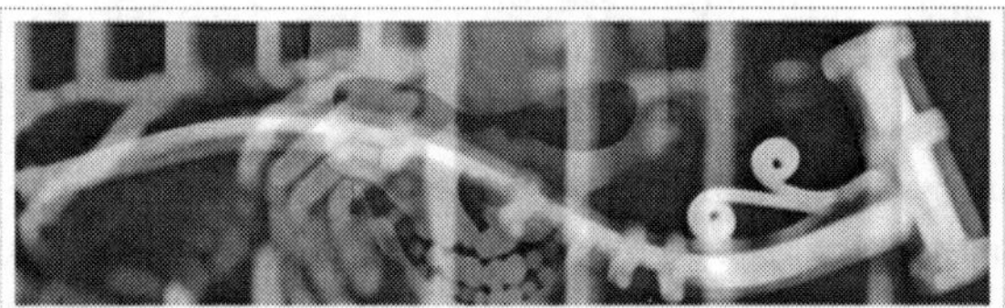

Heroin's Song

I'm sick of singin' Heroin's song
I'm sick of stickin' needles in my arm

Misery is the somber tune
I sing from July 1 through last of June

My every waking moment spent
Composing a lullaby of discontent

My soul scarred with rhyme so sad
Can't remember pleasure ever had

I plead with me to end this song
The lyrics though are far too strong

Sick of singin' Heroin's song
Sick of stickin' needles in my arm

But this tune remains inside my head
Melodies of the walking dead

I sing Heroin's song to cope
Its cords however rob me of hope

Yet still I sing each and every day
I seek but find no other way

For 30 years now, been hummin' this tune
But I'm quittin' again my birthday, the last day in June

I'm so sick of singin' Heroin's song
I'm just sick of stickin' needles in my arm

Billy Holiday, I know why you sang the blues Lady
Kurt Cobain, we must be insane

River Phoenix, Jimi Hendrix, we need a remix
John Coltrane, I understand every note you played

Charlie Parker, Miles Davis
Damned if I know why we crave this

Boy George and Robert Downey,
Janice Joplin, Andy Gibb, John Belushi, Chris Farley,

Big Hump, I miss you…
Lady Day, I know why you sang, I'm sick of singin'
Heroin's
Song; Sick of stickin' needles in my arm

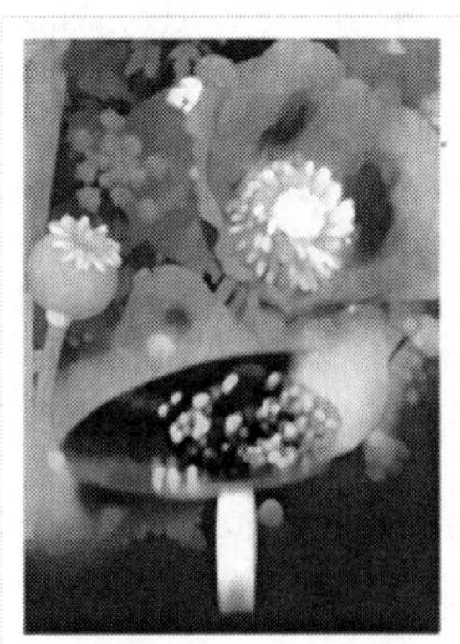

Blown Away

Fall's fallen leaves lay around the base of the tree,
withdrawing…
Sap junkies, all…
Not understanding why the sap stopped running...
Shriveling, shrinking from short sap supply…
Colors, colors simply symptoms…
Emaciated, malnourished, thin things…
Lying around in the gutter…
Craving a shot of sap…
Trembling in the wind…
Terrorized by the leaf police…
As they make their street-sweeping arrests...
Blown away…

Life in a Pipe

I been smokin', tokin', strokin'
My pride's long gone
I been stuffin', huffin', puffin'
Does my ego belong
Lyin', cryin', dyin' in a pipe
All the while
my style
locked in a crack vile
Can't eat, can't sleep
gotta creep
Gotta find that rock
Can't quit it, gotta get it
My soul's in hock
Got me freakin'
and geekin' and seekin'
Think my mind's leakin'
I'm crashin', bashin' and trashin' my life
Haven't eaten
my body's beatin'
Swear this is the last time
Gotta check the microwave
Think I might have cooked my prime
But damn, that last toke was truly sublime
Life in this pipe ain't all it's cracked up to be
I tried…they lied
ain't no tranquility
Tired of life in this Pipe!

"Success is to be measured not so much by the position that one has reached in life as by the obstacles which he has overcome while trying to succeed."

-Booker T. Washington,
Up From Slavery (1901)

Commentary on America's Drug Problem

According to the Executive Office of the President, specifically the Office of National Drug Control Policy, the astronomical use of drugs in the United States cost this country approximately $110 billion annually. Illicit drugs like heroin, cocaine, methamphetamines and marijuana are absolutely destroying the fabric of our society. They are destructive in ways that we often don't consider or that we have become so accustomed to that we push them out of our minds for the sake of our sanity.

Consider how much serious damage is done to Americans annually, even daily, through the use of these narcotics. Crime, accidents, domestic violence, absenteeism, lost opportunity and decreased productivity are just a few of the side affects from substance abuse. Other side affects include high levels of promiscuity among teens, risky sexual behavior and acts of delinquency.

The maximum cost to society is paid in human capital and a plethora of other ways. We pay either directly through death by overdose or indirectly through substance abuse-related sexually transmitted diseases (STD's) like hepatitis, syphilis and HIV-AIDS. Other maladies such as tuberculosis, emphysema, kidney and liver disease are all exacerbated by America's drug habits. The cost to society shows up in ways that we seldom consider as drug related. Think about the amount of traffic fatalities that are directly related to abusing a substance whether it is alcohol, marijuana or a nose inhalant. And what about the effects on the innocent unborn fetus, which if carried to term ends up paying for it the rest of their lives? We are digging our graves with these drugs.

According to the Substance Abuse and Mental Health Services Administration every year since the early 1990's there have been at least 9,300 drug-related deaths in these United States, that's 25 per day or 1 every hour. The National Center for Health Statistics reports that annually there are close to 530,000 drug-related emergency room episodes. That's more than 1440 visits per day or rather, 1 every minute of every hour. The most frequently reported reason for these emergency room visits is drug overdose. And surprisingly the most common motive for the reported overdose is suicide. Is there anyone, anywhere who is willing to address this?

Little Shop of Sorrow

Oh little shop of sorrow please open not your door
please keep your shutters closed
For every time the cheerful soul
sets foot inside your store
he finds the tax of sadness
upon his mind imposed

Drowsiness and laziness serve as draperies in your place
and your shelves are stacked with sorrow
Your inventory is the enemy of the whole human race
and your ledgers forecast no hope for tomorrow

You advertise suffering and pay it to those you employ
then sell it to all who would buy
Your registers swallow up the happiness people enjoy
and your receipts have made the strongest of them cry

The signs upon your walls display heartache
and sore distress
and your windows exhibit only clouds of gloom
Your salesmen barter cheap wretchedness
while the product they package is doom

Yes the soul of the cheerful
must be mindful of your shop
and be careful not to enter in
For we must search for laughter at every single stop
and quench the thirst for gladness within

Our Creator in His kindness has fixed our lives so
that obedience to His law brings blessedness
and the little shop of sorrow is not the place to go
if you intend to purchase happiness

Ode/Owed To Reneé

I remember she was 7
An on-loan angel, from heaven
her smile illuminated rooms
But no way could we have known
that before she was full-grown
her light would brighten only her tomb

No way to predict fate
who at the age of 8
dealt a hand impossible to play
for she was raped and molested
by an uncle who confessed it
For six straight months, every other day

Still Reneé was resilient
her eyes flashed genius brilliant
By 10, seen way more than they should
She'd known a dozen men by 12
which prompted her to delve
way down past the underside of good

Yeah, she smoked and drank and drugged
she robbed and stole and thugged
at 15 spent her last day in school
Now I know you judgmental bigots
sipping from self righteous spigots
laugh and call that child a fool

But this ode to Reneé
is owed to Reneé
she bore the cross of all us saints and sinners
the footstool of the perverted
the ridicule of the converted
playing a game with far to few winners

At 16 she tasted heroin
cause something about the marrow in

her bones caused them to ache
So every chance she got
she'd fill her veins with rot
perchance to ease her pain and her heartache

You see at 8 she had contracted
that virus which abstracted
then taken at least 8 more years to bloom
While her depraved uncle Fester
that scumbag child molester
he died 3 years after sealing this child's doom

So this ode to Reneé
is owed to Reneé
Cause she wore our scars and lived our deepest fears
A scapegoat for the masses
passing disagreeable gases
while crying all our undesirable tears

Yes we owe it to Reneé
to somehow, somewhere, some way
repay her for the hand she was given
and find a way to compensate
for all the scorn and all the hate
encountered each day that she'd risen

For all the pain that she suffered
and the agony she buffered
in search of society's approval
For all the back rooms where she stayed
and all the alleys where she laid
waiting for the garbage removal

So, this poem is a form of penance
while we are serving the sentence
for the crime of murdering Reneé
And I implore each one of you
to pray for her and us too
and pray that prayer every single day
for it is truly owed to Reneé

Domestic Acceptance

(Forgotten September)

He said she just didn't look right
had a sassy gleam in her eyes
so with the back of his hand
this little coward of a man
made evil materialize

He questioned her every move
who she spoke to and where she went
He forbade her club hopping
he stalked her while shopping
clocking how much money she spent

He raped her and called it love making
said she wasn't worth a thin dime
He mentally abused her
and maliciously used her
time, after time, after time

Her friends told her, "girl you're stupid
I'd leave him if I were you
There's no way I would tolerate
all that misery, hollering and hate
you'll be dead before he's through!"

But she loved him and so accepted
his brutal and medieval ways
his verbal attacks
and his backhanded smacks
which confused and confounded her days

Then one morning she finally snapped
she'd taken it for nineteen years
She put a hole in his chest
right through his silk vest
after almost two decades of tears

But now she's upstate doing thirty
for a sunrise she can't remember
still a victim of his violence
which she finally silenced
one forgotten day in September

Written upon request for
Domestic Violence Month-October 2003

Commentary on Anger

According to all the income tax returns filed in 2007, only one-tenth of one percent of American households earned more than $1 million. Now when you take into consideration that we are, by most accounts, the richest nation in the entire world, just this one little piece of information will make you angry as hell, especially the descendents of former slaves in America who facilitated all this wealth in the first place.

We want to know, what happened to our 40 acres and our mules? As I write this in January of 2010, not only is red blood still flowing in Iraq and Afghanistan but red ink as well, to the tune of $114,000.00 per minute. That's a whole lot of change considering there are 1440 minutes in every day. And think about it, all this money is being spent while the gap between the rich-getting-richer and the poor-getting-poorer is expanding.

The poor are so angry that it has become almost commonplace for a person to walk into any public establishment and shoot everyone in sight. "Going Postal" is a term that has been coined to describe this behavior. "Road Rage" is another popular phrase used to depict the levels of hostility fermenting in the country. There was a thing called "Air Rage" spreading up until September 11th 2001. During one week a Judge's family was gunned down at her home. People shooting people in Churches across the country. Another angry individual walked onto a Virginia college campus and killed over thirty people and another shot thirty-one and killed twelve on a Texas Army base. And these are just the incidents that made the national news. America has a violent episode every 4 seconds.

The Center for the Study and Prevention of Violence at the University of Colorado reports: "from 1992 to 1996 the number of murders reported on ABC, CBS and NBC evening news increased by 721%. People are just plain angry. According to the U.S. Justice Department firearms killed 4223 children in 1997 alone. That's one child every two hours. One child is arrested for a violent crime every five minutes; that is 288 arrests per day while almost 10,000 children were expelled from school between 1996 and 1998 for taking guns to class. Between 1985 and 1995 the juvenile arrest rate for murder rose 96%. In 2003 one in three high school students admitted to carrying a gun, a club or a knife to school at some point.

Washington DC, America's capital city has held the nefarious distinction of being the murder capitol of the world on more than one occasion. Most of these murders have been committed by young people on young people. I believe our youth are so hostile because they see what they consider to be undeserving people enjoying life while they struggle to survive. The whole nation saw and heard George W. Bush at a fundraiser (Fahrenheit 9/11) where quite a few of the richest people in the country were gathered as he stated clearly and without any indication of humility that he was happy to be among "the haves and the have-more's."

The problem with that scenario is that there is plenty to go around in America for everyone and if he can have more, then the true laborers should be able to have more as well. Young black people perceive injustices all around them that they are unable to articulate and because they cannot affect change they consider life hopeless and ultimately act out anywhere and everywhere. Sort of like old George W. himself did right after September eleventh. Remember he took the posture, can't find Osama so let's bomb Saddam. I think that may be the start of a poem right there...

Need some place to
Inflict some harm
Can't find Osama
Lets bomb Saddam

What is even more disturbing about the amount of anger displayed throughout America is the disproportionate amount of violence that is reported regarding so-called black African American neighborhoods. According to ABC, CBS, NBC and CNN news, Africans in America have cornered the market on violence. Too often, blacks are depicted in the media as a bunch of savages running around in our neighborhoods robbing and murdering each other. The picture is painted as if blacks are genetically predisposed to commit these violent acts. The media deliberately describes black people as if they were born with an abhorrent flaw that causes them to be hostile. Blacks are portrayed as being hell-bent on destroying themselves.

Now for the sake of argument, let's say all of this reporting was accurate. My question is Why? Why is it like this? Did black people put themselves into these deplorable conditions? How did we get this way? Knowing that a lot of this reporting is exaggerated racial profiling I understand that much of it is designed to psychologically depress and demean black people. There are black people whom I have spoken to who have bought into this brainwashing and believe that there is a violent genetic streak within us as a people that causes us to behave in this self destructive nihilistic fashion and simply cannot help ourselves. This is a lie and a fallacy that must be put paid to and turned on its head. We must at some point come to terms with the notion that in truth, we *are all created equal* and that genetics have nothing to do with our current condition. So how did we come to this point? What is the root of the former slave's present condition?

I'll take an educated guess and say…Slavery! Plain and simple, SLAVERY! Slavery; with all its ugly vestiges. Willie Lynch gave slave owners the blueprint for our present condition on the banks of the James River back in 1712 and as he predicted, there are many of us whom still possess the remnants of that behavior.

Some of us portray and play out according to that prognostication the 'Slave Syndrome, Slave mentality and the abrogation of all responsibility and ownership of one's self with a refusal to self determine and self actualize. That mentality subsists today. I have heard it argued that Willie was a myth and that he didn't actually exist. One thing is certain, if Willie Lynch was only a legend, the myth absolutely exists in our heads and the predictions are displayed in our behavior 300 years later.

Anger is just one by-product of what the real Slick Willie envisioned. Rage and resentment comes natural to most people who have been victimized. When people are used and abused their natural inclination is toward revenge. Hurt people, hurt people. Revenge against an oppressor is a behavioral human constant throughout history. Just look at Nagasaki and Hiroshima after the Japanese bombed Pearl Harbor.

Descendants of former slaves in America are subliminally aware of the fact that their ancestors built this country. They perceive subconsciously that they have been played. They know on a visceral level that the only reason America enjoys the prosperity it does today is because of the free labor it received through the slave trade. Having never been compensated, anger and violence are the nearest things to remedy. Constant disappointment gives way to resentment, irritation, frustration and rage.

Many black people feel an innate sense of rage and don't even know why. We are angry because we understand on a primal level that things aren't right. Deep down we intuitively know that something is wrong, yet we can't fix it or even articulate it. So we act out. Instead of living the same American Dream that we built for others with our own hands, blood, sweat and muscle, we live in projects under clouds of misery, poverty and death.

Just stop and consider what it means to live in a project? It is demeaning, degrading and disheartening. Projects are demoralizing, intimidating, discouraging, scary and downright frightening places to live. They produce demoralized, intimidated, discouraged, frightening and angry people. We are stripped of our morals and principles and then indicted and prosecuted because we don't display any. The proliferation of alcohol, cocaine, heroin and marijuana in our neighborhoods just adds to the demoralization and has decimated them to the point where they are referred to as militarized zones.

My people don't have to go to Afghanistan or Iraq to experience a war zone. Not twenty blocks from where I grew up is Capitol Hill where most of the nation's decision-makers live and work. Yet just a few city blocks from Capitol Hill is Langston Dwellings, also known as 'Viet Nam'. My people live there in abject terror, ravaged by horrors of a real war raging just a few minutes drive from where the symbols of freedom and prosperity stand tall and proud.

It saddens my heart to realize that a nation of such plenty (to date more than $300 billion has been spent on the war in Iraq alone) can be so heartless and cruel and continue to fuel the fires of failure amongst black people. Clearly, these are acts of racism, exploitation and terrorism that the United States promotes and fosters. Nobody; and I mean NOBODY! wants to deal with racism in America, neither the victims nor the perpetrators and racism is the biggest problem we have. Racism is a big giant, stinking mound of waste, festering in the closet of America and nobody wants to touch it.

It's enough to make any descendant of former slaves and true patriot, angry. The problem is so debilitating, corrosive and cancerous that not only black folk are angry, but every nationality in America. I get angry and I write poems. Others get angry and walk into a Colorado high school and blast automatic assault weapons while another does the same on a Virginia college campus. We have 8-year-old children sitting in their living rooms being blown away as the result of drive-by shootings. The fault lies not in the symptom but in the disease. I just wanted you to know why I wrote, "Appeal to An Angry Man."

Appeal to an Angry Man

The same as a tornado tears up trees
and deforms the face of the land
as an earthquake swallows what cities it please
so the rage of an angry man

In fits of passion, anger only sees red
those in its path experience pain
murder, destruction, lots of bloodshed
with no compassion, no understanding, no gain

If you can avoid anger, you are the strong
yours is the strength of God
If you can hold your temper, till the wrath is gone
you will have beaten all odds

A fool is provoked by insulting speeches
but the wise will laugh them to scorn
for the wise are aware that anger only teaches
the tortured, the tormented, the torn

Consider how few things are worthy of rage
What real reasons have you to be mad
The undisciplined usually end up in a cage
repentant, sorry, sad

In vanity and weakness it always begins
but its end is filled with sorrow
on impatience and intolerance it always depends
with no thought about tomorrow

So be mindful of your fury
think again before you shoot
lest you meet your judge and jury
and go to hell in your pursuit

Finally, this appeal, to all of you who care
before your anger harms someone
please say this little prayer
Dear Lord God, please check my temper
keep me calm and cool in strife
raise my thoughts so high that I
could never stoop to take a life

*"Avoid fried meats which angry
up the blood. If your stomach
disputes you, lie down and
pacify it with cool thoughts.
Keep the juices flowing by
jangling around gently as you
move. Go very light on the vices,
such as carrying on in society.
The social ramble ain't restful.
Avoid running at all times. Don't
look back. Something might be
gaining on you."*
-Satchel Paige, *How to
Stay Young* (1953)

Root Out Murder
Put Guns Aside

The United States is unequaled
Murder capital of the world
With an issue facing its people
Destroying its boys and girls

Now the sixth commandment of Moses
States plainly thou shall not kill
Yet some in command oppose this
Murdering citizens at will

With thirty-one thousand killed yearly
More than eighty each day who died
The message is being sent clearly
Cease firing—Stop homicides

Sixty percent of grade-schoolers
Declare frightening news with pride
"Its easy to get a hand-gun"
This horror cannot be denied

While every seventeen minutes
There's a successful suicide
Half of which could be prevented
If we'd only put guns aside

America's great dilemma
A disaster nationwide
We have to ROOT out these murders
We have to put guns aside

Maybe a visit to the morgue
With your son or daughter inside
Would force you to see, finally
We must put these guns aside

How Can You Sleep

How can you sleep nights knowing
the amount of misery you cause
How can your heart rest
after all you have oppressed
breaking both man and God's laws

What manner of creature are you
that destroys life so readily
Just what kind of being
just doesn't mind seeing
pain and suffering so steadily

Wherever you go you demolish
usurp and pillage the land
deplete all its resources
using illegal armed forces
killing child, woman and man

How can you look in the mirror
and account for the evil you do
bombing schools to get oil
Like a lecherous boil
seems even YOU should despise you

When you lay your head to pillow
do you pray as most of us do
And what God could you pray to
that would ever forgive you
for all the suffering you brew

When it comes to committing evil
no one can compare to you
I wonder how you can sleep
and your conscience keep
you resting the whole night through
Just how can you sleep
with all the evil you do

Seriously, How Can You Sleep...

...knowing that you stole the Presidency and was not elected by the American people but selected by your elitist constituency?

...knowing that you entered the office with the strongest economy in United States history and in less than two years, you had every single economic category failing, in the red or headed in a negative direction?

...knowing that within your first two years in office more than 2 million Americans lost their jobs?

...knowing that you cut un-employment benefits for more out-of-work Americans than any other President in US history?

...knowing that you squandered the entire United States Surplus; bankrupted the Treasury and that you and your cabinet set the record for the most personal bankruptcies filed in a 12-month period in the history of America?

...knowing that you set the all time record for the most real estate foreclosures in a 12-month period?

...knowing that you have created the largest budget deficit in American history?

...knowing that you set the watermark for the largest annual budget spending increases than any President in the history of the United States?

...knowing that you set the record for the largest drop in the US stock market in history, including the crash of 29?

...knowing that you presided over the biggest corporate
stock market fraud of any country in
the history of stock markets?

...knowing that you hold the world's record for
receiving the most corporate campaign donations,
from more convicted criminals, than any other President
in US history, and that the largest lifetime contributor
(admittedly one of your best friends) to your campaign
was convicted of one of the largest corporate pilfering
frauds in the history of the world?

...knowing that you presided over the largest energy
crisis in US history and refused to invoke your
presidential powers, even after corruption
was revealed as the cause?

...knowing that all the minutes and records of meetings
attended by you or your Vice President, regarding public
energy policy, are sealed, restricted and
inaccessible to the public?

...knowing all records of your governorship in Texas
have been sealed in secrecy, hidden away
in your father's library and
are not available for public viewing?

...speaking of public records, how can you sleep
knowing that all the files of the Security
and Exchange Commission investigations
into fraud and insider trading of your many
bankrupt companies are sealed in secrecy
and not accessible to the public?

...knowing that all of the minutes of every public
corporation where you served on Boards are also
secretly sealed and not accessible to the public,
under any circumstances?

...knowing that all references and records to your
drunk driving conviction in Maine
have been curiously erased
along with your Texas driving record,
which has also
disappeared mysteriously?

...knowing that your presidency is
closer to a dictatorship
(which you admitted would be easier)
and has the least amount of
Congressional oversight than any in the history
of the United States?

...knowing that since you were selected, Americans
have far less freedom and fewer civil liberties than they
did before you were selected?

...knowing that you have cloaked your presidency in
deception and subterfuge and that you have become the
most secretive, unscrupulous and unaccountable
Head of State in this nation's history?

...knowing that your service records have been doctored,
that you were AWOL from the National Guard, and you
deserted the United States Military during a time of war?

...knowing that you cut health care benefits
for war veterans?

...knowing that in your first year in office, you spent
more time on vacation than any other president in the
history of the United States, which coincided with its
worst security failure ever, September 11, 2001?

...knowing that on your watch, the most heinous attack
in US history took place and you deliberately retaliated
on a country that was not even remotely involved?

...knowing that by doing so you single handedly destroyed US credibility around the world and you now hold the nefarious distinction of being the most hated and protested against human being in mankind's history, including Adolph Hitler?

...knowing that since your selection, you dissolved more international treaties than any President in American history, and your foreign policy is the worst this country has ever had?

...knowing that you are the first President in history to order an attack, with military occupation of a sovereign nation, against the will of the United Nations, the will of the vast majority of Americans and the vast majority of the international community?

...knowing that you are the only President to cause the United Nations to remove America from the Human Rights Commission?

...knowing that you are the only President to slap the United Nations in the face by refusing to abide by the Geneva Convention, disregarding its decisions and withdrawing from the Court of World Law?

...knowing that you are responsible for the worst diplomatic failure in US history, by using the sympathy of the world after September 11th to line your pockets with Iraqi oil?

...knowing that you are the only President in US history to have 71 percent of the European population view you as the single largest threat to world peace and stability?

...knowing that since your unwarranted attack on the sovereign nation of Iraq, tens of thousands of innocent men, women and children have been murdered?

…knowing that your regime practiced psychological warfare on the American people and devised a campaign of terror on the public, more diabolical than anything any foreign invader could conceive?

…knowing that thousands of American soldiers have died senseless deaths, because you arbitrarily decided to bomb a sovereign nation that represented absolutely no threat to the US?

…knowing that you allowed hundreds to die and thousands to suffer due to your negligence and incompetence in the wake of hurricane Katrina?

…knowing that one day you will be tried by the World's Court and found guilty for having committed some of the worst, most horrible, heinous war crimes in the history of the world?

…knowing that for all the above, you should have been impeached?

…knowing that you hypocritically contradict your Christian Right-Wing fundamentalist rhetoric by continuously disobeying the sixth commandment of the Bible? (Thou Shall Not Kill)

Seriously-HOW CAN YOU SLEEP?

Commentary on The Conservative Right

Miriam Webster's *Tenth Edition Collegiate Dictionary*, defines Conservative as: preservationist; of or relating to the philosophy of conservatism; tending or disposed to maintaining existing views, conditions and institutions; traditional.

If you click on the word *conservative* in Microsoft's thesaurus, you'll get synonyms like *conventional, conformist, unadventurous, old-fashioned* and *traditionalist*. When I think about it seriously and dig down as far as I can into my soul, I cannot understand for the life of me how any intelligent person of African decent who has endured the vestiges of slavery in America could consider him or herself a Political Conservative.

What in God's name is it that such an individual would want to politically conserve? Obviously, any descendant of slaves calling themselves a political conservative has not visited the slums of the Ninth Ward in New Orleans, the Crenshaw District of Los Angeles, Langston Dwellings in Washington DC or seen the abject poverty forced upon black people living around 3rd and Mack in Little Rock Arkansas. Any human being who had an ounce of caring in their veins would surely want to change those horrid conditions.

I understand that a few of us want to maintain our nice homes, expensive cars and continue to collect our large paychecks. I don't have a problem with prosperity. I just believe that it doesn't have to continue to come at the expense of my people. We have been America's meal ticket for far too long. Most every creature comfort enjoyed by the "conservative right" has come from the uncompensated labor of the so-called black men and women of America and it is sad and scary to see our people adopt the very philosophy that has kept them oppressed. Conservatives parade a few black affluent folk in front of our faces and say 'see, you have arrived' when the vast majority of us are dying from the stress of not being able to pay this month's rent.

Conservatives have a long history of fighting hard to maintain and preserve its chokehold on affluence in this country. Millions, and I do mean millions, have lost their precious lives so that 'distinguished gentlemen' can continue to sip their mint juleps, smoke their stogies, go hunting at their leisure or discuss mergers and acquisitions on the back-nine at Augusta.

Consider just how far and to what lengths the 'established Conservative Right' will go to stop us from enjoying the American Dream and conserve the status quo. Think about how diabolical those in power have been with their efforts to keep the *haves having and the have-nots, having nothing.* Every time a group of assertive African Americans put their heads and resources together to make a positive change for our people, the venomous snake of conservatism will rise up to put its poisonous fangs into the effort.

Look at the efforts of the Black Panthers and how far the government went to crush their attempts at uplifting our people. From 1968 through 1971, the Federal Bureau of Investigation put on a full court press of infiltration and terrorism. They launched a nationwide campaign to extinguish the organization. Through smear tactics, aggressive character assignations and unlimited financial resources, many conscientious wholesome people who just wanted to see their neighborhoods improve were discredited and placed under blankets of fear. No less than thirty of its members were brutally murdered and disposed of within that 4-year period.

Steven Bartholomew, Arthur Morris, Robert Lawrence, Tommy Lewis and Bobby Hutton were killed. Welton Armstead, Alprentice Carter, Frank Diggs, John Huggins and Alex Rackley were all introduced to the business end of the graveyard. John Savage, Sylvester Bell, Nathaniel Clark, Larry Roberson, Walter Toure' Pope and Spurgeon Winters were savagely murdered. Mark Clark, Sterling Jones, Eugene Anderson, Babatunde X Omarwali, Carl Hampton, Fred Hampton, Fred Bennett, Robert Webb, Samuel Napier, Harold Russell and Sandra Lane Pratt were all taken out by the ruthless regime.

Among the most famous to lose their lives to these conservative efforts were Jonathan and George Jackson. Think about what the impact would be if 30 of the G.O.P's top leaders were murdered inside of 4 years and what that Party would look like. I'm certain there would be blood running in the streets if that took place.

I clearly recall my feelings of despair, when I read about the night of December 4, 1969. The Chicago police shot and killed Mark Clark and Fred Hampton in a pre-dawn raid on their apartment. I was a 17 year-old un-caped crusader for justice who was still reeling from the assassination of Dr. Martin Luther King Jr. Fred Hampton, who was one of the most charismatic of the Panther leaders, was murdered while he was still in bed. That's right, murdered while he slept. It was proven that the FBI had infiltrated the organization all the way to the top. The head of the Panther's security was an agency informant.

Depositions in a civil suit revealed that William O'Neal was working for the FBI as Hampton's personal bodyguard at the time of the shooting. O'Neal gave his FBI contact, Roy Mitchell, a detailed floor plan of the apartment which Mitchell submitted to the State's Attorney's office just hours before the pre-dawn terrorist attack. According to FBI agent Roy Mitchell's affidavit, Fred Hampton's bodyguard was paid $10,000 for his information. There is a whole mountain of evidence regarding these and other horrifying, repulsive and horrendous acts committed by those who would conserve the elitist privileges enjoyed by rightwing powerbrokers in this country.

Consider how far America will go to put down any perceived threat to status quo in the case of Malcolm X. It has long been thought that Malcolm was murdered by former friends and colleagues who were members of the Nation of Islam. According to popular belief he was killed because he split off from the NOI and formed his own organization called Muslim Mosque Incorporated. What is seldom revealed is the tremendous amount of effort and money that was spent by the government's Federal Bureau of Investigation to cause the rift between Malcolm and the Nation of Islam. If murder is paid for doesn't it make the Employer (Commissioner) complicit by virtue of its commission?

The split was as a result of 'Cointelpro' (America's Counter Intelligence Program) at its finest. Again, there is a huge pile of evidence unearthed under the 'Freedom of Information Act' that clearly demonstrates how both organizations were infiltrated and summarily brought down through the tactics of the 'conservatives' who would, will and still murder to maintain the status quo. Think about the following information that is not made readily available to the general public.

Malcolm was supposed to have been murdered by his former friends as a result of the factions that sprang up inside the NOI. However, the factionalism didn't just spring up out of the ether. It had been conceived, coerced, paid for and implemented by the FBI using covert and overt strategies hatched right at the very top of the Federal Bureau of Investigations; a part of which was to ignite the divide and conquer strategy and rend the foundation of the organization igniting bitter and spiteful debates within.

Through COINTELPRO there was a massive campaign of rumors and innuendo that tarnished the names of Elijah and Malcolm. The smear tactics ultimately put them at odds with each other, which activated and advanced internal disputes between the members of both groups.

The Chicago Special Agent in charge of the Nation of Islam's destabilization, Marlin Johnson, who coincidently oversaw the assassinations of Mark Clark and Fred Hampton, makes it painfully clear that he believed the murder of Malcolm X would be a model for "successful counterintelligence operations." (See FOIA-No.80-2229 or 657 F.2d 140)
He states in an affidavit, "Over the years considerable thought has been given, and action taken with Bureau approval, relating to methods through which the NOI could be discredited in the eyes of the general black populace or through which factionalism among the leadership could be created. Serious consideration has also been given towards developing ways and means of changing NOI philosophy to one whereby the members could be developed into useful citizens and the organization developed into one emphasizing religion, the brotherhood of mankind, and self-improvement. Factional disputes have been developed, most noted being Malcolm X Little."

There's an avalanche of information that clearly demonstrates that Malcolm was taken out by those with resources that far exceeded the capabilities of Elijah Muhammad and the Nation of Islam. And for the reader who has respected my opinion enough to read this far, let me tell you that in my heart of hearts, I knew then, just as I know now, that it was the United States Government in all its sovereign glory that brutally gunned down (Al Hajj Malik Shabazz) Malcolm X Little.

Now let's pay closer attention to how Conservatism assassinated Dr. Martin Luther King Jr. An internal FBI monograph, dated September 1963, http://www.icdc.com/~paulwolf/cointelpro/churchfinalre

portIIIb.htm revealed that because of the tremendous support the Civil Rights Movement had been attracting the preceding five (5) years, civil rights agitation represented a clear threat to "the established order" of the United States and that Martin Luther King Jr. was growing in stature daily as the leader among leaders of the Black movement…"so goes Martin Luther King, so goes the Negro movement in the United States."

This was the view accepted wholly by COINTELPRO specialist William C. Sullivan who wrote shortly after Martin's I Have a Dream speech: *"We must mark King now, if we have not before, as the most dangerous Negro in the future of this nation from the standpoint of communism; the Negro and national security. It may be unrealistic, to limit our actions against King to legalistic proofs that stand up in court or before Congressional Committees."*

If the above statement is not a preamble to assassination/murder, then I really don't know what is. If it is 'unrealistic, to limit your actions against King to legalistic proofs', then, what is your plan B; what is realistic? What is beyond the limit of legalistic proof? Annihilation? Assassination? Murder? Who was the real villain here? Was it some single racist zealot or was this a governmental decree to dismantle the movement towards racial equality?

Martin Luther King Jr. and the SCLC simply organized because they were tired of being brutalized as people. So they came together to secure voting rights for those who were disenfranchised across the rural and urban south. They were ultimately trying to dismantle the blatantly racist aspects of segregation. However, rightwing conservatives in the FBI saw this as a threat to the U.S. government and national security. That is a question we should ask ourselves today, in 2010. Is racial equality a threat to the United States? To those who would posit that we have racial equality because we have a black president, I say, hogwash.

In September of 1957 FBI supervisor J.G. Kelley forwarded a newspaper clipping featuring the formation of the Southern Christian Leadership Conference to the bureau's Atlanta field office. The memo that accompanied the clipping instructed local agents that the civil rights group was "a likely target for communist infiltration," and that "in view of the stated purpose of the organization, you should remain alert for public source information concerning it in connection with the racial situation."

The Atlanta field office did more than just follow instructions; they opened a COMINFILE (Communist Infiltrated Group) and launched a full-fledged investigation. That investigation ultimately led to the first-degree murder and assassination of Dr. Martin Luther King Jr.

I point these issues out because it seems to me that instead of wanting to conserve this way of life, we should be trying to reform it. Instead of conserving it we should be repairing it. So what about reparations instead of conservation?

©

"My father was a slave and my people died to build this country, and I'm going to stay right here and have a part of it, just like you. And no fascist-minded people like you will drive me from it. Is that clear?"

-Paul Robeson, testimony at *House on Un-American Activities Committee* (1956)

What If Reparations

What if we decided
we had to be paid
for the days we labored
and the days you played

What if African Americans
demanded their due
for all those conveniences
provided to you

If we stopped right now
took a real inventory
how good people
would you defend this story

From sunrise to sunset
working in the fields
dying from exhaustion
and hardly any meals

What if my people
demanded their share
of the prosperity enjoyed
from their wear and tear

What if we commanded
a monetary commission
for all those stolen
patented inventions

Alexander Mils invented
the elevator
would we be paid by steps saved
or paid by each floor

How much money
do you have lying around
cause he gave you the means
to get off the ground

Richard Spikes invented
the automatic gearshift
was that paid for, I wonder
or was that a gift

And how much cash
could you have driven to the bank
if you never had
good old Richard to thank

And Garrett A. Morgan
invented the traffic light
but all compensation
has been stolen outright

Has Garrett's family prospered
like those of Alexander Bell
I think not, I think
their repayment's been hell

Elbert R. Robinson
invented the electric trolley
but seeking remittance
is considered folly

His invention led
to the modern day bus
but were any of those proceeds
paid to us

Because of Charles Brooks
America's streets are cleaner
but his offspring could not
have been treated any meaner

Now this list could go on
till the cows came home
cause we even cooked you steak
where the buffalo roamed

But I'll end this now
with this one question again
What if? What if you just paid us
what you owed us, my friend?

From Cain't See to Cain't See

(A Slave's Freedom Poem)

From caint see to caint see
I work'd the fields
From caint see to cain't see
got muscles o' steel

Work'd from the rising
till the fallin' of the sun
when sick and hurt
got no sympathy, none

My back you branded
my chest marked too
till all my dreams
'bout stranglin' you

Cause you took my child
and sold him away
and raped my daughters
two times today

You traded my mama
for a Kentucky mule
then called me a savage
and my daddy a fool

My uncle you hung
for tryin' to leave
but he the lucky one
got a early reprieve

You slept on satin
whilst I wallowed in mud
and whipped my back
till its covered in blood

Called me nigger
knowin' it weren't my name
drove me to drinkin'
and my daddy insane

From caint see to cain't see
sun up to sun down
you buried my spirit
my soul you drowned

And all your improvements
from southeast to northwest
came from the treasures
in your slavery chest

The bridges and the roadways
and every side street
was tarred and paved
under the soles of black feet

From cain't see to cain't see
you work'd us like oxen
Mischief's what you is
a poison, a toxin

And the more I reckon
how you worked us to the grave
the more I figure
you is depraved

Said the good book
had decreed it so
all slave request
be answered with no

So from sun up to sun down
from cain't see to can't
every straight path
you gave a crooked slant

You used my wife
to warm your bed
then forced my daughter
to cradle your head

You tarred and feathered
all uppity slaves
said "that'll learn us all
how to behave"

And I guess the main thing
that makes it so sad
is your evil heart
ain't never felt bad

bout all that misery
dealt by your hand
Monster's what you is
you ain't no man

'cause how could a man
from sun up to sun down
work another man
into the ground

Yeah, from cain't see to cain't see
that's been my plight
but this here runaway
Is freed tonight
And I bet you didn't know
that I could read and write
this here poem…ha, ha, ha…

"We have come over a way
that with tears has been watered,
We have come, treading our path
through the blood of the slaughtered."

-James Weldon Johnson,
Lift Every Voice and Sing (1900)

Commentary on The Confederate Flag

White supremacists argue that because the Confederate flag is a part of America's history it should be allowed
to fly anywhere. I wonder if the people who support the Confederate flag's flying in America would also encourage flying the Nazi flag over provinces in Germany. After all, it was a part of the Germans' historical make up at one time. I wonder if those same people who want to maintain the antebellum antics of the slave-traders in this country would sit still for the flag of the British United Kingdom hovering over their heads. Why start the history with the Confederate Flag? The British Union Flag preceded the crossed stars and was certainly hoisted high over this country for a long time. Or better yet, let's bring back the *Skull and the Cross-Bone* flags of the various pirates that raped, pillaged and raised their banners over America.

Racism is alive and well in America and shall continue to thrive until we can enter into serious discussion about the mindset of those who would keep us enslaved. That mindset is to conserve the customs, culture and traditions of the Confederate States of America. A confederation that was born and propagated on slavery, racism and white-supremacy. It was propped up and promulgated by greed and total self interest of an inhuman and evil philosophy predicated by a mindset of people who were willing to die rather than admit that all humans are created equal. This is the definition of conservative-ism at its root and most ruthless. There are conservatives today who would like to roll back the advances to embrace this agenda and reinstate their world vision of entitlement and subjugation of all peoples who are not THEM! Looks like THEM or has their DNA. This *conservative* attitude clings viciously to the premise that certain human beings are to be classed as undesirable and considered only three-fifths human because they have more melanin/pigment in their skin than the stock of pure-bred Caucasoid or the Hitlerian-Arian, northern European Anglo Wasp.

In 1861, the Vice President of the Confederate States of America, Alexander H. Stephens stated, that the belief of the Confederate government is: "The Negro is not equal to the white man; that slavery (subordination to the superior race) is his natural and normal condition." Evidently, Mr. Stephens was not aware that just a few decades before his naïve and egotistical statement, Caucasian people were learning about culture and refinement from the Moors in Africa. Neither could he have known that less than 200 years prior to his misinformed statement, his ancestors were considered savage and bestial by the great civilizations of Africa. The fact that so-called superior white people were just emerging from the dark ages obviously was not in his frame of reference. And I really wish someone would explain the connection between the preamble of the U.S. Constitution *"All men are created equal and endowed by their Creator with certain inalienable rights,"* and the Confederate Constitution; *"The citizens of each state shall be entitled to all the privileges and immunities of citizens in the several states, and shall have the right of transit and sojourn in any state of this Confederacy, with their slaves and other property; and the right of property in said slaves shall not be thereby impaired."* How can a man be equal and a slave at the same time?

America is in a terrible state of denial when it comes to race relations and slavery. Nobody wants to face the horrors and holocaust of the slave trade and the deep injurious wounds it inflicted on the country. That part of our history we want to gloss over as if by doing so such flagrant denial will ease the pain or erase the scars from history. I have heard people say things like, "why do African Americans always have to bring up slavery?" Or, "I'm not responsible for what my ancestors did; that was then, this is now." Well denial will never solve any problem much less one as enormous as chattel slavery. And please forgive me for being naïve here but the responsibility has to fall somewhere.

If millions of humans suffer as a result of my mother's and father's behavior and if as a result, I continued to prosper from their ill-gotten-gains, then wouldn't it be my responsibility as a human to do all I could to at least acknowledge the issues and search for a means of restitution, reconciliation or correcting the damage done. That should be the responsibility of all human beings in the 21st century. Relations between blacks and whites will never get any better until we face up to these facts. Skeletons never stay hidden in the closet. Eventually we all have to face the truth. Every horror film ever produced showcases the fact that ill-treated ghosts never lay dormant forever, they always come back to haunt the perpetrator.

America was built on the backs of slave labor. America owes all of its prosperity to the African American slaves who designed, constructed and maintain this country. So-called White Americans owe so-called Black Americans a tremendous debt. There is such a thing in the U.S. as "Silent Depression" as was pointed out in 'State of the Dream-2009' which can be read at www.faireconomy.org and this depression is direct result of that Debt.

The sole reason America has enjoyed such prosperity as a country is because it has never had to pay for its labor. NEVER! The reason America is and always has been an economic force is because the economy was built on the backs of slaves. If I could take 100 acres of cotton to market and never have to pay for the labor associated with that endeavor, I'd be in pretty good shape and so would my offspring. How many thousands of percent and how many times has the interest on that initial 'free ride' to market compounded, enfranchising the offspring of the enslaver and disenfranchising the descendants of the enslaved? I challenge the reader to Google "Texas Troubles" and read how eighty acres of land was given free and clear to every white man who brought a slave to Texas during the mid-1800's.

Americans should consider this, indeed the world should consider it. Think about how you feel when you're in the presence of a bully or someone who takes advantage of others. Unless you are a bully yourself, you know how bad that makes you feel. Well just imagine having a bully take advantage, misuse and abuse you for over 300 years.

So, why is the issue of the Confederate Flag such a sticky one with African Americans? Why can't we just leave it alone and let it wave away? Because its like that bully. Why? Because it is an oppressive, offensive slap in the face of all African Americans and black people around the globe. To have that flag waving feels the same as a rape victim would feel if the rapist continually waved his soiled and diseased underpants in the victim's face. It is the same as having the swastika emblazoned on every public building and being saluted by holocaust deniers and Nazi sympathizers. It's the same as bringing back *whites-only* water fountains and *strange fruit* dangling from southern lynching trees, fruit that rotted on the vines because we believed the preamble of the United States Constitution.

Why won't the issue go away? Because it's like a tumor eating on the body of the state; without treatment it festers and grows. We see the symptoms everywhere. The crime and violence acted out on the streets, in the homes, in the workplace and in the schools of America are indicators that the system is flawed, flawed with denial, the longest river. We need to talk, people we really need to talk!

"If we accept and acquiesce in the face of discrimination, we accept the responsibility ourselves and allow those responsible to salve their conscience by believing that they have our acceptance and concurrence. We should, therefore, protest openly everything that smacks of discrimination or slander."

– Mary McLeod Bethune, *Certain Unalienable Rights* (1944)

We Must Never Forget

(A Poetic Case for Reparations)

Denial is the longest river
its current always destroys
its shallow banks
refuse to give thanks
while exclusion and rejection's employed

Now America has a problem
accepting the facts as they are
facing slavery's truth
is repulsive, uncouth
and makes for an ugly memoir

Cause you traded in human beings
branded us like we were cows
then sold us like cattle
like no more than chattel
these facts you cannot disavow

And with all those acts of evil
you reveled in celebration
While you brutally castrated
we steadily donated
our blood, fertilized your plantations

You raped us, lynched us, butchered and burned
denied our human rights
we were tarred, feathered, skinned and spurned
you worked us by day and by night

In every aspect of industry
you thrived off the fruits of our labor
From apples to zinc
we've been the link
through slavery, America's been favored

Socially, educationally, economically
you flourished while we were denied
yet, if it weren't for us
this country 'd be dust
its commerce would surely have died

And for this you say you won't pay
won't even apologize
But why should you pay the debt
that your forefather's let
Cause you prosper from all their lies

Indeed, "we must never forget,"
That's a phrase we should all preserve
concerning lives that were lost
in the Jew's Holocaust
and that's no more than we deserve

So why should we forget ours
when monuments are built to theirs
Are they superior, are we inferior
Were theirs better than our forebears

And please remember good people
their tragedy was on foreign soil
but the bodies of slaves
are in American graves
yet, few tributes to our turmoil

America you'd best wake up
cause Lazarus has risen from the gate
Pay the debt you owe
so the country can grow
and learn how to love 'stead of hate

We want our acres and our mule
You've had yours for generations
Now its time we were paid
from the fortunes you've made
its time for slave reparations

And we must never forget!

"Tell them that the sacrifice was not in vain. Tell them that by habits of thrift and economy, by way of the industrial school and college, we are coming. We are crawling up, working up, bursting up: coming through oppression, unjust discrimination and prejudice. But throughout them all, we are coming up... "

Booker T. Washington, *Up from Slavery*

Deferred Dreams

I dreamed of a home where the grass was green
my neighbors were happy and pleasant
But I woke to streets of asphalt so mean
only fear and despair were present
MY DREAM WAS DEFERRED

I dreamed the schools taught children to think
and the system encouraged our youth
But curriculums didn't have the missing link
and some books taught lies not truth
ANOTHER DEFERRED DREAM.

I dreamt that crack never entered my hood
and the eyes of my people were clear
But I woke to merchants up to no good
selling five dollar rocks right here
ANOTHER DEFERRED DREAM

I dreamed king heroin lost his throne
and my folk regained their pride
But I woke in the projects, hooked on bone
and my pride, was set aside
YET ANOTHER DEFERRED DREAM.

I dreamt that murder was a thing of the past
and weapons had disappeared
Yet I woke to a generation dying fast
with gunshots loud and clear
STILL ANOTHER DEFERRED DREAM.

Finally, I dreamed it was all a plot
that my deferment was contrived
But when I woke, the reward I got
was the knowledge I had survived
IN SPITE OF MY DEFERRED DREAMS.

"What happens to a dream deferred?
Does it dry up
like a raisin in the sun?"

-Langston Hughes, *Harlem* (1951)

In Spite Of...

The fact that I was not allowed to read…
Said my thought capacity was incapable, inferior…
My mental ability to assimilate and discriminate faulty, you said...
"Slothful," you called me…
Due to a genetic flaw, related to Ham's indiscretion…
But here I am in spite of…
Being separated from my father and taught to hate my brother…
Cause he's cursed, you say...
Systematically removed any cultural memory I might have…
Stole my customs-stole my traditions…
Said it was white when it was black…
Black when it was white...
Yet here I am in spite of…
Segregation, discrimination, aggravation, humiliation…
Mutilation and even castration…
Still my determination has me here…
In spite of…
Turned my spirituality against me…
Got me searching the sky for pie…
Yet here I am looking at you, eye to eye…in spite of…
In spite of…
Believing a servant was worthy of his hire…
Never being paid for my labor…
Never paid me for my pain and suffering…
Never paid for all those God awful years…
Never paid me for my sweat...
Blood…tears…
Yet here I am…in spite of…
In spite of…
You stealing all my inventions…
You men of leisure…
All my labor saving devices…
You men of leisure…
My time preserving devices…

You men of leisure...
In spite of…
You taking all the credit…
You men of leisure…
I am still here…
Flourishing…
In spite of…

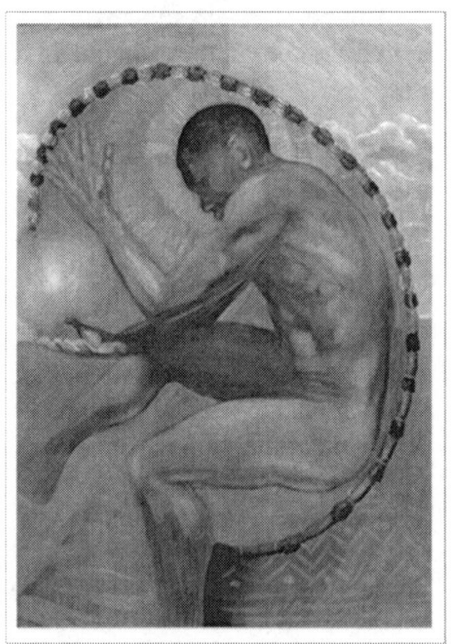

"You have seen how a man was made a slave; you shall see how a slave was made a man."

-Frederick Douglas – *Narrative of the Life of Frederick Douglas* (1845)

North Wind

I'm battling a north wind that blows
cold on my warm African Ancestry…
A north wind that tried hard to snuff out
my invaluable contributions to civilization...
I'm fighting a northern wind, whose icy ideals
would bury my African manhood
under a European *avalanche of misinformation...*
A north wind that chills aspirations
and forces them to wear a heavy coat of apathy…
A cold wind that cares nothing
about the concerns of citizens…
A blustery, heartless wind…
A bloodless, gutless wind that freezes
and squeezes life from all in its path…
A night wind that steals the souls of the trusting…
An ill wind that blows no good…
I'm wrestling a north wind that tried
to blow away my pride...
I'm rumbling, as Muhammad Ali rumbled… A northern
wind that hit below the belt after the bell rang…
A wind that kicked me when I was down…
A northern blizzard of big white lies...
A wind that blew a veil over my Jesus,
whited him out and placed icicles
'round his philosophy...
A deceptive wind that tried to blow
the light out of Africa,
and make it the *Dark Continent…*
An Oliver North wind that blew crack cocaine
through the lungs of the lost 'round my way…
A gale force wind that whisked heroin through the veins
of the disenfranchised…

A cold relentless wind lurking
round every corner liquor store…
A greedy wind feeding off the feeble and the needy…
A seedy wind that simply does not care...
I'm battling a northern wind that blows out light and
extinguishes hope's fire...
The key phrase remains, "I'm battling!

Liberty Miss Liberty

Rising in the harbor of America so great
Built on a platform of apartheid and hate

Standing for justice so straight, so tall
Justice for some, not justice for all

Using the wretched refuse of your teaming shore
Prospering from the labor of your tired and poor

Balancing on the shoulders of so many slaves
Sending human cargo to painful early graves

Huddled masses yearning to breathe free
Tasting the bitter bark of the lynching tree

The chains of oppression you promised to break
You slipped around the ankles of the slaves you make

You raped my daughters, my wife you abused
My sons you hung by the neck confused

Stripped me of my God and changed the Good Book
You altered my name, my pride you took

Huddled masses yearning to breathe free
Guess that line didn't apply to me

Yet still Miss Liberty, I believe in you
And pray one day, you'll believe in me too…

September 2000

"I felt that one had better die fighting against injustice than to die like a dog or rat in a trap. I had already determined to sell my life as dearly as possible if attacked. I felt if I could take one lyncher with me, this would even up the score a little bit."

-Ida B. Wells, *Crusade for Justice: The Autobiography of Ida B. Wells* (1970)

Commentary on 18 Missing Years...

What happened to Jesus after he turned 12 years old? Where did he go? Who did he live with? What did he do? How did he do it? What did he learn? What did he teach? Why is there no mention of him in the Bible for 18 years after he turned 12 until he turned 30?

It is my humble opinion that the single most devastating blow to the melanised people of the world is the theft of the identity of Jesus the Christ. That Jesus was African/Hebrew has been so well documented by noted historians that only staunch racists in abject denial try to argue in this day and age that Jesus was a pale-skinned, light-haired, European. Scholars from Cheik Anta Diop to Dr. John Henrick Clarke have written volumes proving that Jesus
was born and raised in Africa, his parents were African, he was educated and worked in Africa and he lived and died in Africa.

Jesus is arguably the single most influential human being ever to have lived, at least as far as this western civilization is concerned. His influence is vast and far-reaching and permeates throughout our society. We call Jesus' name for everything. When we're in excruciating pain, we invoke the name of Jesus. Jesus this, Jesus that. When we're at the very pinnacle of pleasure, again, we call to Jesus. In crisis, in fear, in jest we call Jesus. I believe his name has been repeated more often than any other name in the last 1700 years, within the Western hemisphere.

The legacy and genius of Jesus, along with his identity, was stolen 325 years after he walked this earth and the evidence is there for all to verify independently if one is so disposed by simply researching unimpeachable

documentary evidence that is readily available to all interested souls. The Emperor Constantine instigated this in Nice, Italy at the 'Nicene Council' in the year 325 A.D. He and his learned scholars and fellow rogues concocted a scheme of propaganda for the explicit purpose of advancing their agenda that would serve to demoralize and brainwash the entire civilized world for the next 1700 years. That scheme was simply to claim all responsibility for, and take ownership
of Jesus' identity. The same Romans who murdered him systematically destroyed all literature and accurate artistic depictions of him. They declared that Jesus was God Himself and that the Pope was his closest representative on earth. The irony in this is that Jesus adamantly opposed anyone worshiping him or anything other than Almighty God. He also vehemently denounced the priesthood declaring that human beings did not need other human beings to intercede between themselves and God.

He taught that God was opposed to showy displays of piousness with fancy robes and gaudy hats. He was clear on his position that worshiping idols and shrines had nothing to do with holiness. *And Jesus said, "0ur God must loathe the tinseled show of priest and priestly things. When men array themselves in showy garbs to indicate that they are servants of the gods, and strut about like gaudy birds to be admired by men, because of piety or any other thing, the Holy One must surely turn away in sheer disgust. All people are alike, the servants of our Father-God, are kings and queens. Will not the coming age demand complete destruction of the priestly caste, as well as every other caste and inequality among the sons of men?"* Aquarian Gospel – Ch: 35 Vs. 8-11 Yet I ask you to look closely at the rituals of the Roman Catholic Church with its fancy robes, countless statues and shrines. It appears to go directly against the instructions left by Jesus.

Here is another clear indicator that the ethnicity of Jesus has been tampered with over the centuries. From the years 685 to 695 and then again from 705 through 711A.D., the Emperor of Rome was Justinian II. During the first 10 years of his rule, he had a coin minted that depicted Jesus with straight hair and Euro-centric features in line with Constantine's decree. He must have had an epiphany because during his second reign he had the coin changed to depict the actual African image that he found consistent with the early Byzantine Church This depiction denoted thick lips, wide nose and curly, locked-hair with clearly Africanized features. See J.A.Rogers Sex and Race Vol. 1 pg. 292

In the catacombs under Rome there are black paintings and statues of Jesus, the Madonna and other biblical characters to this day. In the hard-to-find classic, Anacalvpsis, historian Godfrey Higgens writes on page 138, "the God-Christ, as well as his mother, are described in their old pictures and statues to be black. The infant God in the arms of his black mother, is himself perfectly black...the whiteness of the eyes and teeth, and the studied redness of the lips, are very observable." Yet the Roman Catholic Church undertook massive crusades plus the Inquisition to rid the world of any knowledge of this melanised Jesus. Torture with cruel methods of dismembering and decapitation were used to dissuade any who tried to preserve the true African/Hebrew identity of Jesus. As a matter of fact history records that the Inquisition was among mankind's cruelest and most inhumane periods ever in the history of the world. The Judas Chair, the head vice, stretching the body on the rack and burning at the stake were just a few of the many torture methods used by inquisitors. Helen Ellerbe in her book *The Dark Side of Christian History* states, "There has been no more organized effort by a religion to control people and contain their spirituality than the Christian Inquisition. Developed within the Church's own legal framework, the Inquisition attempted to terrify people into obedience. As the Inquisitor Francesco Pena stated in 1578, 'We must remember that the main purpose of the trial and execution is not to save the soul of the accused but to achieve the public good and put fear into others.' The Inquisition took countless human lives around the world as it followed in the wake of missionaries. And along with the tyranny of the Inquisition, churchmen also brought religious justification for the practice of slavery."

As late as the 20th century in Vatican City the Office of the Inquisition was still one of the churches most powerful branches until 1965 when Pope Paul VI renamed the Inquisition as the Congregation of the Doctrine of the Faith. A rose by any other name…

Another attempt at the theft of Jesus' identity is the long debated *Shroud of Turin.* The shroud was supposedly the burial cloth Jesus was laid to rest in after his murder. It was proven false through DNA testing and carbon dating which demonstrated beyond doubt that the shroud (a cloth with an image of a straight-haired, sharp-featured Eurocentric type) did not exist during the fourth crusade in 1204 A.D., proving that it could not have been used to wrap the body of Jesus, as it was manufactured more than 1200 years after his death.

"Something like the Turin Shroud could have been created by an artist without the slightest fraudulent intent, the artist's concern being solely to represent the Passion drama in the cloth's stains in the most graphic and instructive form." Writes Ian Wilson in The Mysterious Shroud (1986).

Here is another attempt to paint Jesus as a pale face. According to legend St. Veronica stepped forward to wipe the sweat from Jesus' brow as he suffered through the Passion on the way to Calvary. Her towel, (Veronica's Veil) which was alleged to have miraculously changed into a holy icon after touching his brow, was also instantly transformed with his image embedded into the cloth forever. It also portrays Jesus as having the facial features of a European. This is yet another ploy to perpetuate the large, as opposed to, little-white-lie surrounding the personality of the African Jesus.

Artist' renderings of a blond-haired-blue-eyed Jesus were distributed throughout the world by zealots and missionaries. "*Altogether there were more than forty rival claimants for the title of 'Holy Shroud' and the claims of every one of them have been minutely examined by historians. Yet in only one case – that of an isolated reference dating from 1203 – is there any possibility that it might have been the Litey or Turin Shroud. In all the other cases the dimensions are completely different and, most significantly of all, in no instance (except in that 1203 reference) is there any mention of a miraculous image. In other words, alleged shrouds of Jesus may have been relatively thick on the ground, but in almost all cases they were blank pieces of cloth.*" – Lynn Picknett & Clive Prince, *Turin Shroud – In Whose Image? The Shocking Truth Unveiled* (1994)

The missionaries did such a thorough job of brainwashing on the continent of South America that almost every other male child is named Jesus. (pronounced Hay-Soos) This brainwashing was so exhaustive, so complete and permeating, that people still believe to this day, that the Pope is a holy figure closer to God than any other being on earth when in fact all of Jesus' teachings emphatically state that anyone claiming to be closer to God than anyone else is a liar. Matthew 23:9 "Call no man your father upon the earth: for one is your Father which is in heaven." Jesus' own words clearly state that no person needs a middleman to God, we are, each one of us, our own priest. It makes you wonder if the Pope has actually read Matthew 23:9

Having grown up in the Roman Catholic Church, I experienced and have observed first hand, this brainwashing. In every one of my family members' homes and indeed most of the homes of my friends, there were icons, statues, figurines and pictures of this straight haired European who was supposed to be Jesus. The favorite of course was Michelangelo's depiction of Jesus in his famous painting, The Last Supper, displayed inside the Sistine Chapel. There are some who claim that the portrait is actually a painting of his sister. I don't know about that, but I do know that as a child I remember a lot of kneeling and genuflecting to these idols on a daily basis.

I don't remember ever being comfortable in the Catholic environment, as if my soul knew I did not belong there. I now understand the far-reaching psychological effects that kneeling and kowtowing behavior had on my self-esteem. Imagine having little to no contact with any Caucasian people in your everyday existence but having this figure placed high above you everywhere you go. Imagine believing your entire life that the Lord looked nothing like you. Imagine living in fear and having to look up to your former slave master. Imagine being forced to call someone Father who really wasn't..

I would sincerely ask the reader to stop right now and imagine, no matter if you are black or white, that for the last 500 years the image of Jesus looked like Danny Glover or Isaac Hayes. Stop what you are doing, close your eyes and just think what a difference that would have made on this entire planet.

Nothing would be the same. I remember when I first found out that Jesus was of the true blood of the ancient Moabites and Canaanites and a descendent of Africans. I remember how my heart soared and my self-esteem rose like a phoenix from the ashes. I wrote a formal letter to the Catholic Archdiocese renouncing Catholicism and its sexually deviant life style. To this day I am more confident and productive with the knowledge that I can accomplish the same feats as Jesus. As soon as I realized that he looked like me, I no longer had the inclination to abuse my body through the use of alcohol, heroin, tobacco and other harmful drugs.

It is amazing what heights one can scale if he or she feels good about himself or herself. My morals and principles improved because suddenly I had a most excellent role model. Suddenly, Jesus did not appear to be the enemy who harmed, enslaved and misused me, or represented those who raped and pillaged my people throughout our history. Instead, I envisioned him as a true and divine prophet of God, an African, my brother, my friend, the son of God and a connection to my Creator. At the same time, I discovered why, in my opinion, the 18 most formative years of his life were systematically removed from the Bible.

I have made inquiries, petitioned and even begged priests, nuns, pastors, deacons, reverends and many astute scholars of all denominations of the church to answer just one question. What happened to Jesus after he turned twelve, up until he turned thirty years old? Why is there no mention of him in the New Testament at all? Why are there eighteen consecutive years missing from his life's work? I offer for your reflection the findings of the Reverend Cain Hope Felder, Ph. D Professor of New Testament Languages and Literature at Howard University in
Washington DC.

"What Color Was Jesus? We can now return to the question of the race of Jesus of Nazareth. His mother Mary was Afro-Asiatic and probably looked like a typical Yemenite, Trinidadian or African American of today. Consider a few inescapable factors that challenge the traditional perception of the Madonna and Child. In Matt. 2:15 and Hos. 11:1 we find the words, 'Out of Egypt, I have called my son.' The passage is part of the notorious flight into Egypt, which describes Mary and Joseph's attempt to hide the one that King Herod feared would displace him. Imagine the divine family as Europeans hiding in Africa! This is quite doubtful.

(Egypt has always been part of Africa, despite centuries of European scholarship which has diligently sought to portray Egypt as an extension of southern Europe. Literally hundreds of shrines of the Black Madonna have existed in many parts of North Africa, Europe and Russia. These are not weather-beaten misrepresentations of some original white Madonna, but uncanny reminders of the original people who inhabited ancient Palestine at the time of Jesus of Nazareth and earlier. The 'Sweet Little Jesus Boy' of the Negro spiritual was in fact quite black. Mary, Joseph and Jesus were neither Greek nor Roman. With the marvelous oils and watercolors of the painters brush, the world gradually witnessed the rebirth of Jesus, as medieval and Renaissance artists made him suitable for the portrayal of Christianity as a European religion. Thus there developed a brand new manger scene, with the infant Jesus and his parents re-imaged. Ancient darker, and clearly more African, icons were discarded or destroyed. Many in the 1990's who think of a black Jesus as an oddity or scandalous distortion of historical facts insist that Jesus was Semitic, or Middle Eastern. However, to call Jesus Semitic does not take us very far, because this nineteenth-century term refers not to a racial type, but to a family of languages including both Hebrew and Ethiopic. About the same time that the European academy coined the term Semitic, it also created the geographical designation called the Middle East – all in an effort to avoid talking about Africa! This academic racism sought to de-Africanize both the sacred story of the bible and Western civilization. There is no reason for anyone who loves and respects the truth to take offense at the conclusions drawn from our studies and annotations that Africa/Eden was the stage upon which the biblical stories were acted out, by actors who happened to be black." – The Original African Heritage Study Bible-King James Version (1993)

Now arguably, we are discussing the single most important figure in western society. How could the years be missing in the first place, and more importantly, why are they not to be found in the Bible? President Richard M. Nixon had 18 minutes erased from his presidential life and the country became outraged. If we remove eighteen years, especially those formative years, from anyone's life, we have a problem. But we're talking about Jesus, the man upon whose shoulders the entire civilization rests according to many Christian faithful. And guess what the most consistent answer has been to my question. It's unimportant!—the things Jesus did when he was 21 years old do not matter. What he went through at age 27 do not merit reflection. I was told that we have all the information we need about Jesus. God gave us just enough for us to get into heaven in the Bible. And when you raise the subject about ethnicity the standard answer has been that this is not important either. They profess that it doesn't make any difference what color he was because the only thing that is important is the message he left and the work that he did.

Let us examine this idea for a second. If Jesus' ethnicity and color is so trivial and means so little in the overall scheme of things, then why on earth would anyone go to such great lengths to change his identity? If his true identity and ethnicity is so unimportant, then why was such painstaking effort taken to make him appear as a European, when in fact he was African? Why would a man of African extract, who lived and worked and even sometimes hid among Africans, be always portrayed as a blond-haired, blue-eyed European? Why?

Let us now briefly explore what Jesus did during those so-called "unimportant" eighteen years. At twelve he left home (the Judean Hills, Africa) and traveled to India where he lived amongst the Sudras. The Sudras were considered and are still to this day treated as the lowest class of citizen in the country of India. These people ironically are the richest in pigment that India has to offer. Their skin is as dark as any on the continent of Africa. Not only did Jesus live and work among them, but he also hid among them on many occasions when his enemies were looking to do him harm. There are numerous accounts of Jesus' many years spent in India. There are stories of how Jesus stood in crowds while people inquired of him and the inquirer could not distinguish Jesus from any other Sudra.

Likewise, there are numerous accounts of the many years Jesus spent in Egypt. As a matter of fact, as a sidebar, where in the world is the Middle-East and when did Egypt leave Africa and go to the Middle East? I have heard of Continental-Drift but this Country-Drift is something else entirely. Remember the designation 'Middle East' did not exist prior to the nineteenth century and has been used ever since as a geographical/political identifier by people with a political, social and psychological agenda to destabilize and disorient the less educated. And please keep in mind that during the time of Jesus what appears on today's maps as the Middle East appeared then as Africa. Except for a man-made canal, that whole area was, is and evermore shall be Africa. Pardon me, but some things are just plain ridiculous if you give them serious consideration. The people of India and Africa are dark complexioned, melanin-rich people and if Jesus could live, work and hide among them, then he certainly had to look like them. So again, why would any people go to such great lengths to change this obvious truth? "Hair of lambs wool and feet of burnt brass" are not European characteristics. Rev. 1: 14 & 15 Yet, if these physical characteristics are not important, again I ask, why go through such troublesome alterations and who would benefit from making such modifications?

My point is that the men and women referred to in the bible were primarily black African people. Moses was an Egyptian whose hand turned white and then black again under an unusual set of circumstances (Ex. 4:6,7) Black Sampson , the Nazarene, had dreadlocks before Delilah cut his hair. (Jdg, 16: 17-19) Solomon declared that he was black and comely. Simon was a Canaanite and according Acts 21: 37-39 Paul was mistaken for an Egyptian. Chief among these biblical figures was Jesus.

All of his fore-parents were African/Edenic. Abraham, Boaz, Ruth, Jesse, King David, Solomon, Hezikiah, Joseph and Mary, all were black African. I could go on and on talking about this subject because of the profundity of its nature. I'll just leave you with the poetic answer my soul gave me after no one else could tell me what happened to those "18 Years".

18 Years

I searched my soul
for the truth to unfold
the mystery concerning the Christ
It said, "you my son
are the victim of one
elaborate conspiracy, a heist"

Take a good long look
at your holy book
carefully, prayerfully observe
Through someone's intention
Jesus is not mentioned
for 18 years, not one single word

Then my soul dictated
it was Jesus who stated
"Know the Truth, it will set you free"
Yet, if 18 years are missing
somebody did some twisting
someone didn't want me to see

At the age of 12 he traveled
and began to unravel
the mysteries of life and death
From 12 till he was thirty-three
he grew strong and sturdy
teaching truth about the Holy Breath

So the question in my mind
if you would be so kind
as to indulge me in my brief bit of glory
WHY – why would 18 years
of his blood, sweat and tears
be extracted from His Holy Story?

And when the answer came
freedom did reign
it actually set my soul free
for it finally revealed
what had long been concealed
simply, Jesus was a black African like me
I said Jesus was a black African like me!!!

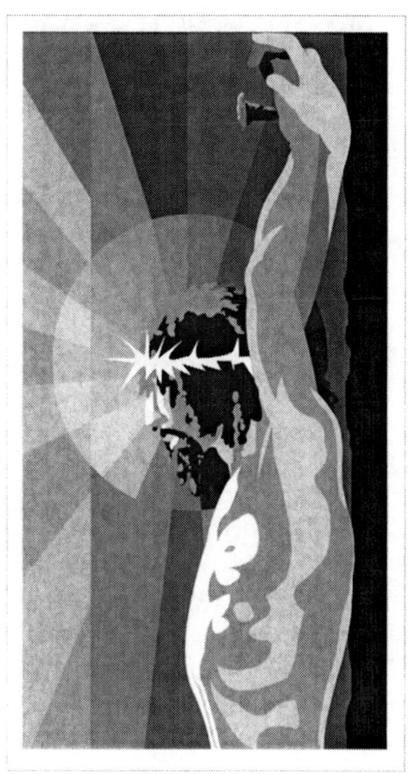

Commentary on Over There—Life after Death & Judgment Day

I was born with Scarlet Fever. Back during the 1950's, scientists still had not gotten a grip on the disease and lots of people died. My mother and father had two sons before me. They are buried in Arlington Cemetery because my dad was in the Army at the time. Neither of my brothers lived beyond 6 months of age. I too, was born with the fatal disease and was not expected to survive past my sixth month, however I did, but for the first 7 years of my life I suffered from periodic fevers.

Today, 40 plus years later, of all the memories I have of my past, this particular one is far and away the most vivid. I remember one day, in my seventh year, I was stricken with fever so terribly that my mother called an ambulance, terrified that she was about to lose her third and only surviving son. I recall her bending over me with an ice-filled washcloth and applying it to my forehead in an attempt to keep me cool. She was crying her eyes out. Of all my memories, this is the clearest.
I recall these next few moments as if they were yesterday. We lived in a one-bedroom tenement walkup off Benning Road in northeast Washington D.C. I can vividly remember leaving my body on a thin white thread that looked like a filmy see-through umbilical cord. I was lying on a couch in our living room. I rose from my body as mist would rise on a foggy morning at daybreak and floated up to the ceiling.

When I got to the ceiling, I looked over at what I still recall as the most beautiful site I have ever seen to this day. I remember colors of bright, cloud-like blues, deep lapis blues, magenta's and magnificent gold. I could see a light that was electrically alive and totally indescribable. The light was pleasant and serene. It seemed to emit peace. I was stricken with awe. I recall my breath catching in my chest and I was humbled. I smiled and looked back down at myself lying on the green hideaway-couch that served as my bed in our living room. I looked at my mother's tears, running down her cheeks as she agonized over the thought of losing her last and only child. I said to her, "Ma, stop crying. You're going before I go and there's nothing to cry about. It's beautiful over here." I can still see the way she looked up at the spot where my soul seemed to be hovering. She had this quizzical look on her face, as if she heard something, but was not quite sure what it was. I'll never forget that look on her face. Then, I looked back at paradise. That's the closest word I can find to describe what I saw, paradise. It was the most incredible site you can imagine.

In that instant, I came to the realization that there is no death. There is existence after this earthly experience. I have proof, intangible proof within my heart and my soul. My proof lies in the very thoughts I am transferring to this paper. I cannot grasp these words physically, no more than I can put a grip on my soul. Yet, you and I know they both exist as surely as you are contemplating these phrases. I had an episode (an out-of-body experience) that transcended my flesh. I had the pleasure of visiting beyond. I am totally convinced that life continues after what we perceive as death. In fact, I believe there is no death. Nothing dies, it just transforms. That experience is part of the reason I was prompted to write: "Over There" and "Judgment Day."

Over There

I left my body on a thin white thread.
Scarlet fever pronounced me dead.
I drifted thru the ceiling, far overhead.
These are the words the Master said,
"There is no death!
There is no death!"

On an old green couch my body lyin',
Ma's tear drenched face above me cryin',
fearful she'd witness yet a third son dyin',
struggling to revive me, God, she was tryin'.
She didn't know,
There was no death!

I visited a place most haven't been,
saw wondrous sights most haven't seen,
what stood out most is, all was clean,
immaculate, spotless, faultless, pristine.
A voice said,
"Over there, there is no death!"

Colors of royal blues and gold,
high-light the greatest story ever told,
I observed the dawn of peace unfold.
A voice said, "My son behold,
There is no death!
There is no death,
over there."

I longed to go yet it wasn't my time,
had rivers to cross, mountains to climb,
essays to write and poems to rhyme.
I was far too young, still in my prime.
Step off Scarlet fever, I come to declare,
there is no death…
Over There!"

April 2002 forty-three years after the episode…

Judgment Day

What will your life style be worth on judgment day?
Is your lifestyle one that helps those in need,
Or does your life style exhibit selfishness and greed?
I wonder what that will be worth on judgment day?

Is your life style one that cultivates life's flowers,
or are you about the business of making sweet sour?
Will it be worth it that day to hear the Lord say,
"You never did my work, all you did was play."
I wonder what that'll be like on judgment day?

What will it be like, if the record reflects,
for the hungry and the homeless, he had no respect?
What will it be like, if on your tally sheet,
it says, "All he ever did was lie and cheat?

What will it be like on judgment day,
if on your report, there's nothing good to say?
"He had lot's of money, trinkets and gold,
'but his ticket to Heaven, I think it was sold."

What will it be like to have it said,
"His tongue had a fork in it, of the truth he was afraid.
He had a chance to save a life, but instead he took it,
Did everything he could, to make the straight path
crooked."

"Why, he had every creature comfort one could think of,
house was filled with everything, everything but love."
"But you could count on him, to be there
in times of trouble,
only if your trouble, meant he would profit, double."

"And he was real quick to flatter, to him it didn't matter,
to him it was something of a sport."
Or what if it was written, that he spent his life getting',
but in giving he was always short.
What would it be like at judgment
if all this was on your report?

Will Your Life Style Be Worthless On Judgment Day?

The Devil Left This Evening

The devil left this evening
with a bulge in his pockets
left one slumped over the bathtub
left one with bulging eye sockets

Yeah, Satan he left this evening
with a smile on his face
He left big John's baby sister
with just a little taste

"I can't leave you much-o-this lil' girl
cause you might O D on me
We got a whole lot more of this dope to twirl
and I need you, back here by three"

Old Lucifer he left this evening
but he left the neighborhood chained
He left with his pockets bulging
and an army of junkies trained

Oh yeah, he left this evening
but I'm afraid he's comin' back
first thing in the morning
with a fresh new batch of crack

The devil left this evening
he looked just like Miss Maggie's son
You've seen him in a lot of neighborhoods
you know, the nice looking one

That devil he shot poor Bobby
about three weeks ago
said he was hurtin' his business
disruptin' his cash flow

Yeah Satan, he reigned with terror
over all that he surveyed
Confident in his arrogance
that he would never be played

But he left extra early this evening
and the word spread he was dead
It seems poor Bobby's mother
put three bullets in his head

Yeah, the devil left this evening
and I guess this time for good
But you'll find him alive and well
in another neighborhood

Church Search

My family applied lots of pressure
forced me to go to the church
but my spirit was missing a measure
cause I'd always leave there in search

Empty and feeling half hungry
longing more food for my soul
divided, confused, in a quandary
torn between opposite poles

The statues they forced me to worship
had no power to answer my prayers
still they pushed and coerced me to worship
idols unfeeling, unfair

So I left home looking for answers
in bottles and cans and pills
suffering from spiritual cancer
but drugs had no cure for my ills

I worshiped false gods of material
got lost in stuff and things
puzzled, bewildered and prodigal
singing songs the miserable sing

Then I stumbled unsure to this doorstep
fearful and frightened and scared
But God whispered, "Son, take one more step
your way has been prepared

The spiritual food you're craving
is plentiful, abundant inside
your place, the Pastor's been saving
your prayers have been applied"

Now I worship and praise the Father
thanking God for sending His Son
knowing I need look no farther
no longer the prodigal one

The Lord brought an end to my church search
He made what was coarse quite simple
And now my vision is clear
He was leading me here
I was searching for Reid Temple

One Man

If one man would make up his mind
to everyone he meet's be kind
and fix his heart on that which is true
If one man would be so bold
as to embrace the gospel and hold
just think what a million men could do

If one man changed his thought
each time the tempter brought
some selfish scheme that would his neighbor undo
If he thought for just a minute
just where is the kindness in it
just think what a million thoughts like that could do

If David could slay that giant
though huge and extremely defiant
and Solomon had the wisdom to think things through
If Shadrach could walk through fire
and his entire village inspire
just think what a million Shadrach's could do

If Noah could build that ark
though some people thought it a lark
and Jesus could cure those deaf and blind men too
If Sampson's strength was that of ten
ordinary men
just think what a million Sampson's can do

If Muhammad could move a mountain
And cause rocks to spew like fountains
And Drew Ali could start a movement true
Just think what a million of us could do

If one man would take a second
when his needy neighbor beckoned
and followed literally Moses' tenth command

With spirits filled and nourished
our neighborhoods would flourish
how quickly peace would spread throughout the land

If one man made up his mind
to no matter what, be kind
No matter what others might put him through
The strength of that man's resolve
would all our problems solve
And just think what a million men like that can do

Commentary on Death by Decision

I want to tell you a story about a small town with a one-lane bridge that anyone entering or leaving had to cross going in or out. One fine autumn day, when the sun was high and the air was crisp, a gentleman who had been out of town on business was making his way back. As he approached the bridge he saw that the 'Grim Reaper' was about to enter the city limits.

At first he panicked, started to do an about face to run for his life when, just as suddenly, guilt set in as it dawned on him that all of his family, friends and loved ones were inside. So he hesitantly approached the graveyard emissary and asked him why he was going into his town. "I'm inclined to go in and take 100 with me," said the Undertaker.

The man was about to plead with Death not to take his folk when he realized that it would be futile because it was evident by the look of Death that the Prince of Darkness had made up his mind. Rather than plead with the Reaper, in a flash of inspiration he ran ahead of Death and knocked on the doors of his family and friends to warn them of the imminent danger, shouting, "run for your life, run for your lives, Death is coming, Death is coming. He says he's taking one hundred. Death is coming, Death is coming."

At the end of the day, the exhausted fellow returned to the spot at the mouth of the bridge where he first encountered the Dark Emissary. With head hung low and a heavy heart he asked, "Why did you lie, you said you were only taking 100 and more than a thousand died? Why did you lie?" Death's response was, "I'm not to blame for the 900 hundred extra who perished. My duty and bond was to claim 100 and so I did. As to the surplus, why it was you, good sir, who applied the stress. For they did not die by my devices, they were frightened into my realm. They worried themselves into early graves. So please don't blame me, blame your feeble expectations."

The good citizen hung his head in shame and walked away. This short story prompted me to pen
Death by Decision.

Death By Decision

Death approached the city's gate
One single lane bridge to cross
With plans to seal one hundred's fate
and ten times ten souls be lost

As one good townsman returned home
the Reaper conveyed his plan
to make the blood of a hundred foam
and add to his deadly clan

"Please gruesome fate, could you not
feast on my folk today
Please cast your net on another lot
Please take your coffins away"

"Negative sir, to your request
my job is the taking of lives
To this task, I do my best
On dread and destruction I thrive"

The townsman quaked, and so he ran
alarming all he could fear
"Run for your lives, fast as you can
Death's Grim Reaper is here!"

By day's end, one thousand died
the good citizen quite confused
questioned Death, as to why he lied
and why nine hundred more were bruised

"I never lied, I did my job
your panic was not my vision
You, good sir, provoked that mob
and their death, was your decision
"Their death's was your decision!"

Commentary on Anthrax

The poem that follows was written about a month or so after September 11, 2001 when the country was in a furor concerning terrorism. Not only had airplanes been flown into the World Trade Center in New York City and some sort of apparatus flown into the Pentagon outside Washington DC, but someone had sent lethal doses of anthrax poison to various Post Offices around the country, and people died. Two of the victims worked at a new postal facility built in Washington DC. As a result, it was evacuated and all of its employees were instructed to go to hospitals and get an antibiotic antidote called Cipro. The newscasters showed people lined up at hospitals and clinics like it was the plague at the end of the world.

It was a frightening time. Living and working in Washington DC was extremely stressful. People were in panic mode. Senate buildings were shut down, streets rerouted and some folk were moving to the mid-west to get out of "Dodge". And the media- the media bombarded the airwaves. Adding insult and panic to injury, two snipers were running around the Nation's Capital killing people. Radio, TV, the Internet and Newspapers were flooded with terrorist threats and color codes of yellow, orange and red. In my opinion the media did far more damage to the American psyche than the actual terrorist ever could. Every waking moment was filled with negative news about some threat or another. It seemed as though the media did the terrorists' job more effectively than they had done themselves. Radio and television broadcasted so many negative news stories on anthrax that they prompted me to write *Anthrax Blues.*

Anthrax Blues
(Postal Workers Nightmare)

Sitting here sipping on Cipro cocktails
aching from the loss of my brothers
terribly terrified touching mail
frightened for the lives of others
I got the Anthrax Blues.

I'm a carelessly categorized carrier
working on the last plantation
Uniformed in a gray-blue barrier
sickened from a city's citation
I truly got the Anthrax Blues

Terrorist telling too many tales
to too many tarnished taletellers
they're far too many souls for sale
by far too many sellers
I'm aching from the Anthrax Blues

My facility closed and fastidiously fumed
for spores spontaneously spewing
While letters laden by larcenist loom
a Death Witch's brew a brewing
I really got the Anthrax Blues

My impugned immune system impulsive implodes
from antibiotic nervous contractions
While viced, viral, vitamins virtually erode
My skin's having an allergic reaction
I'm sick of these Anthrax Blues

Somebody tell the caster
of the late-breaking news
I'm tired of hearing them singing
these Anthrax Blues

October 2001

"9/11 Kamikaze"

Confused irises widen
Hearts palpitate witnessing obliteration
Breathless
wandering 'round reason
Peripatetic nomads drifting rootless
cross destruction's desert
say "all must die!"
"All must die!"
Sanity on hiatus
Minds locked, bound in cargo holes
crammed with puss, venom and hate
"You shall suffer the slings and arrows"
Miserably seeking the company of annihilation
Strapped to two hundred thousand pounds of steel
Sipping ignited jet-fuel
while gobbling and guzzling the fire
We welcome you to hell!
Kamikaze…

11 September 2001

Winged Hatred

Hatred on the wings of a 767
in a New York state of mind
declared, "I have my orders, and on nine-eleven
I'm disrupting all mankind"

And my brother, loathing
Wrapped in a missile's clothing
will head for the Pentagon
with thorough instructions
to rain down destruction
till your families and friends are gone

You see my mission here
is to instigate fear
and I shall not be ignored
Seeds of evil and dread
must be planted and spread
till panic and horror is restored

Because Hatred's my name
Terror's my game
and you see, I just gotta play
Thus your prayers and songs
plus your hum-a-longs
will never stand in my way

Cause the enemy we're seeking
is not somewhere sneaking
'round some middle-eastern mart
Our biggest foe
Congressman, Senator Joe
is your cold and calloused heart

21 September 2001, ten days after
the Twin Towers imploded…

Future Doubt

Sprawl and crawl, please help me y'all
the earth is straight degrading
Doom , gloom, there's no more room
the ozone layer is fading

Global warming, new diseases forming
population out of control
gangsters hoarding oil, while river water's spoil
Dear Lord, save our souls

Gas prices soaring, preacher's sermons boring
and Enron's off in the Bush's
Martha Stewart lying, while K-Mart's dying
Las Vegas' taking no more pushes

Mad cow disease, designer herpes
on the brink of nuclear explosion
whole planet shrinking, septic tanks stinking
beaches got a cousin named erosion

Hurricanes more severe, increasing each year
tornadoes leaving mass devastation
plant life we're losing, while concrete we're choosing
bringing on deforestation

Hell, we don't need no trees, we don't need no breeze
living on carbon emissions
got so many cars, we're leaving earth for mars
checking Map Quest for road conditions

Natural environment, headed for retirement
been given an early out
social security, a forgotten obscurity
future, seriously in doubt
OUR FUTURE'S SERIOUSLY IN DOUBT!!!

April 2004

Ain't You Tired

Ain't you tired of your hip-hop generation
bein' a dyin' population
victims of self-annihilation
Sellin' dope to one another
keep killin' your brother
no respect for each other
Ain't you tired

They call you generation X
but what has me perplexed
is what's comin' next
The only muscle you flexin'
is one that keeps vexin'
your own

Exploitin' your sister
You pimpin' her mister
raisin' her skirt
causin' her hurt
diggin' up dirt
Who you think it hurts
some white boy named Curt

Ain't you tired
of sirens in your hood
that mean you no good
but the bars understood
On your knees shootin' crap
who's really the sap
Ain't you tired of this rap

Ain't you tired of attendin' funerals
regular as roman numerals
Fillin' up caskets
like church collection baskets.

Aint you tired of being 21st Century slaves,
diggin' your own graves
They say you depraved
and cannot be saved
Ain't you tired of actin' like beast
Don't you at least
want to preserve your own

Aint you tired of...
Your mothers and sisters cryin'
cause their baby boys are dyin'
and ain't nobody tryin'
to correct it.

Undertaker sighin',
Policeman lyin',
Your life they ain't tryin',
To protect it.

But you keep on shootin',
your own, you keep lootin'.
Keeping your race dead last.
Ain't you tired,
of your generation dyin' so fast?
Ain't you tired?

Teach Them

Our children leave school yearning
because life-skills they're not learning
There's a gap, a void, a problem, there's a hole
To fill it, schools must be
institutions of integrity
above all else, truth must be told

Our children are rebelling
because the truth we are not telling
History class strips them of their pride
If we want them to excel
historical truths we must tell
protocol and politics aside

If we want our young to learn
their respect we must earn
To stop violence schools must teach the truth
Teach them race pride, give them hope
a reason they should cope
You'll see a fundamental change in all our youth

Teach them a sense of their self-worth,
that they're the pride of God's good earth
The violence will stop virtually over night
if they are proud of their ancestors
they'll be proud future investors
buying stock in everything that's right

We have the chance to save one
but we must be the brave one
with courage to alter, courage to make a change
Our current methods are failing
There's an air of despair prevailing
We must change before they're all estranged

Finally, we have to raise their self-esteem
to restore that bright-eyed gleam
They have to know how great they were before
If they take pride in their great past
they'll start learning fast
Then our greatness and our splendor they'll restore
But we must teach them...

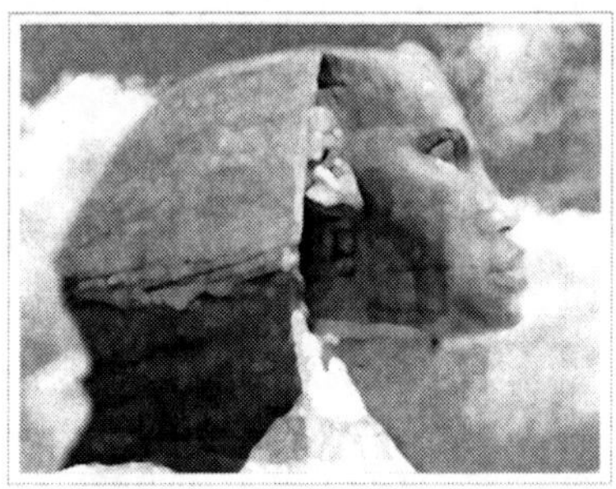

"The question is not whether we can afford to invest in every child; it is whether we can afford not to."

-Marian Wright Edelman, *The Measure of Our Success* (1992)

Labels

They slapped a label on me
said he's dysfunctional at best
and with the stroke of one hand
placed a negative brand
then ran a battery of test

They said you know he's special
his brain doesn't work like ours
It's wired all wrong
so he can't get along
has deficient mental powers

They said he's slow to learn
and his wit's a little dim
Said he's just a buffoon
we'll be rid of him soon
don't worry too much about him

It's as though they marked my forehead
with a flashing sign that reads
he's the Jack of all Fools
with no thinking tools
they're cruelty made my soul bleed

And the labels they kept on coming
like Retard, Idiot-Savant
ADHD, Bipolar
just zap him with Zoloft
that's all he really wants

Then, after 17 years of crying
sighing and dying inside
one who could see
beneath the surface of me
had the nerve to turn the tide

This child's been misdiagnosed
his thoughts race faster than yours
and it was your labeling
which caused his disabling
and all his mental detours

His words were liberating
cause I never dreamed I was able
Now life's taught me 2 lessons
One is never think less than
The other is…never LABEL

The Keys

She begged and she pleaded
Convinced me she needed
To take a short drive to the mall
Please give me the keys dad
Relax rest at ease dad
Just meeting some friends that's all

A small voice in my head
Whispered softly and said
Don't give her the keys today
But I paid little heed
Cause I knew she would plead
Plus whenever she drove I'd pray

Plus she gave me that look
Which was all it took
Whenever she wanted her way
And for sixteen years
With either laughter or tears
She could shape and mold me like clay

So with a wink and nod
And a feeling quite odd
I dropped the keys in her palm
Nodded out in my chair
With hope and a prayer
And enjoyed my afternoon calm

But an ominous tone
Rang through the phone
Just around two hours later
A voice said: "Mr. Gray-EL sir
I have bad news to tell sir
Your car has been found in a crater"

"What's sad and perplexing
Is your child was seen texting
Focused not on the road, but her phone
And I'm sorry to say sir
That she's passed away sir
She will not be coming home

Then my brain overloaded
And my heart exploded
As I dropped to the floor on my knees
You have to be dreaming
A voice was screaming
Why did you give her those keys

Now since my heart attack
I can't seem to get back
To a place where my mind is at ease
Cause I can never forget
And shall always regret
Handing my daughter those keys

Bless the Day
(Where Would You Be Without Us)

If it weren't for Lewis Latimer
in the dark you'd be
cause he placed that filament
in the light bulb you see

And you'd better walk softly
as I give you this news
it was black Jan Matzingler
that laced up your shoes

Now this poem is written
with deliberate intentions
To question your position
without the Black man's inventions

Cause I wonder if you'd be driven
to treat Black's right
knowing that Garrett A. Morgan
invented the traffic light

I wonder if you realize
You could not ramble
without that super charged turbo
invented by Joseph Gambol

And without Richard Spikes
let me tell you my dear
there would be no driving
without his automatic gear

And this whole world
would be stuck on the first floor
without Alexander Mils'
first elevator

At this point I must give
Benjamin Banneker a chime
he hand-crafted a clock
so you could tell time

While we're at it
he deserves another pat on the back
cause I know you know
he invented your Almanac

I wonder if you'd enjoy
as much fun and folly
without Albert R. Robinson's
electric trolley

And this one fact
might cause you some pain
Granville T. Woods
invented almost near everything on the train

And evidently Charles Brooks
believed he was his brother's keeper
Why on earth else
would he invent the street-sweeper

William Barry invented the post marker
and William Purveys the hand stamp
While George T. Samon's dryer
stopped your clothes from being damp

And you men of letters
owe William for his fountain pen
And you gotta thank a brother
for that Cotton Gin

You would freeze to death
without Alice Parker's
heating furnace
in your home

And what would your head look like
without Walter Samon's comb

And I know you'd be in a terrible mood
without J. Standard's refrigerator, cooling your food
Where would you be without us
I could go on and on
If I were you, I'd bless the day
the Black man was born

Appreciation for Granville T. Woods

I'm trying to figure out
where America would be today
If Granville T. Woods
didn't invent that electric relay

And how come I never heard of him
when I was in school
Who decides who's important
who makes those rules

Cause Granville T. Woods
should be immortalized
He was the first to use
electricity-polarized

For inventing the phone transmitter
he receives no credit
from all our history classes
his name has been edited

America's railway system
will be forever in his debt
But I haven't heard him mentioned
in a classroom yet

This brother invented
the electromagnetic brake
but this fact has been hidden
for racism's sake

Granville's machine was first
but few will admit
he was the first one to make
the telegraph transmit

The galvanic battery
and the railway telegraph
we owe to Mr. Woods
Teach that in the class

And how many others
has racism fooled
by keeping such knowledge
out of our schools

Cause I ain't never heard
of Granville T. Woods
and with more than 50 patents
don't you think that I should?

February 1998, written for my alma mater elementary school class African History Month program

Calling All Rappers

I'm calling all Rappers to get involved
Calling all MC's, we need this problem solved
The problem is, what we're saying
It's time for us to stop fakin' and playin'

Cause I don't need to know how many women you got
some respect for your sisters would help your race a lot
I really don't care 'bout your diamond Rolex
when the same time is kept by a Timex

So you got a Benz, so you got a truck
the majority of us don't give a _____!
You stuck on your gear, and stuck on your threads
While we need some self-love up in our heads

If you're really stackin' chips as fast as you say
let's put some of 'em where they'll truly pay
I'm calling all Rappers, I hope you can feel
this life ain't no joke, this life is for real

While we're killin' each other and beefin' bout nothin'
some blue-nose in a board room, on a cigar puffin'
"those Negroes you know, are intellectually pathetic
but I sure am glad they're so athletic!"

I'm calling all MC's to help me out
I know you got sauce
I know you got clout
But at this moment your future's in doubt

Let's rap about something
making economic sense
'Cause all y'all know
we been straddlin' the fence

What if we rapped about stocks and bonds
and buyin' houses and mowin' lawns
and takin' good care of our African Queens
teachin' truth to our youth, and providin' means

I'm calling all MC's, let's take charge
Let's learn to love self, that's livin' large
If we rap about unity and sticking together
we change the political climate forever

Why we keep beefin' anyway
I think we been tricked,
let's fix it today
Let's rap about takin'
back our streets
give the devil back his dope
cause it only defeats

our purpose you see
stunts our growth
I'm callin' all MC's
to take this oath

"Most of my rhymes
will be the upliftin' kind
dropping straight lyrics
that stimulate the mind

raise up our people
not put 'em down
If I can't say somethin' good
I won't make a sound"
Respect…

Respect the Flow

(O G Rapper's Prayer)

Thought I'd write this flow
Just to let you know
this game didn't start with y'all
I've been puttin' down rhymes
since before your time
Winter, Spring, Summer and Fall

You see I started to spit
when the world was lit
and my Father said "let there be light"
I spoke the beginning word
I'm sure you've heard
He ordained my skillz be tight

So as keeper of the flame
and protector of the game
I gotta keep it sucka free
'cause the lames will defame
the playa and the game
and blame all their shame on me

I got no time for dissin'
Cause I would be missin'
the play and the flavor'd be gone
I find what's right in a dude
try and never be rude
and like moths to a flame he's drawn

I look for something good
up under a playa's hood
cause we're members of the same lodge
I appreciate his cipher
got no beefs to die for
and no hot balls to dodge

See a true playa is one
who has stopped hatin', son
with no deliberate enemies
he drinks no hater-ade
knows that hatin' is played
and prays for his frien-emies

When he's writing rhymes
he ain't wasting no time
tryin' to be harder than he ain't
cause he knows full well
once locked in a cell
most of them hard talkers faint

Thought I'd write this flow
just to let you know
I got love from back in the day
I respect your skill
and I always will
and I pray for you every day
Respect…

My Pain Rose

My pain rose like that geyser at Yellowstone
it was old and faithful
yet it leaped and spit and spewed
all over

My pain rose
It rose like the dust rose
from the World Trade Center
cementing thousands under clouds of anguish
My pain rose
with prickly thorns protecting its crimson beauty
it stung and hurt and maimed, it tortured
it was old and faithful
like that geyser
hot and humid and cloying

My pain rose
to greet me at sunrise
issuing forth edicts
from the great State of Depression
It rose to full mast
like the flag over the Pentagon
the day before September eleventh
My pain rose early, every daybreak
needing no vacation
gray and gloomy like fog
it rose

My pain was a ventriloquist
manipulating me like a wooden dummy
to herald its preeminence
It rose from agony's bowels
a deep wound

It rose like water rises, seeking its own level
It rose and bobbed its ugly head
like empty bottles on a stream
It rose and lingered and stank
like breath from stale beer

My pain ached, like a decayed bicuspid
throbbing on jangled nerves
My pain rose
and has risen every morning, like clockwork
since the day after you left me… Rose

Trapped

In a web of untruths and deceit,
playing a fruitless game of denial,
as if my eyes lied.

Trapped,
Caught under an avalanche,
of useless gifts and perverted truths.

Ensnared,
by your obstinate refusal to face it,
It is over…
The showering of offerings which once were sweet,
have become cloying, tainted, useless, trinkets,
tarnished by your infidelity.

Treed,
with no way to descend down the branches,
of broken promises and leaves of disappointment.

Pinned,
down under a cornucopia of faithlessness, disloyalty and
betrayal,
as if my eyes lied.

Entangled,
and knotted forever umbilically,
by the life we produced.

Immovable and fixed as you believe yourself to be,
I need you, only, to set me free,
for I am,

Cornered,
as a wounded mammal,
protecting its young.

If Caged,
birds really do sing,
this one lost its melody.
I need my wings,
wings you,

Clipped,
with your faithless, adulterous, treachery.
Please open the snare,
of your,

Trap,
for it is over!

What Happened to the Passion?

What happened to the passion
that used to be
seen in most eyes
as we struggled to be free

When Malcolm could ignite us
cause our blood to rush
and Martin, with one word
the multitude would hush

I wonder where the passion went
When we had a cause
did our passion go in peace,
with the passing of some laws

Has the flame of our passion
been blown out by drugs
or was our passion stolen
by some corporate thugs

What happened to the passion
that once prevailed
even though you knew
protest meant jail

Was our passion checked
at the door with our coats
or was our passion strangled
by the gold 'round our throats

When we marched for freedom
what was it for
To give it all back
at the designer store

What happened to the passion
in our neighborhoods
What happened to our quest
for the common good

What happened, can you tell me
Please explain
Did our passion leave
on a west bound train

Or has that one-eyed Lucifer
called the TV screen
sucked our passion into it
drained us clean

I wonder where our passion went
Does anyone know
If you find it, please tell me
'cause I miss it so

September 1997

Where in the World is the Negro?

If all people get their names
from the land whence they came
and that's the way we're all identified
then there's a whole country missing
some geographical twisting
just where on earth did Negroes reside

If every sovereign nation
is named for its location
and the people called according to their land
then how on earth is it,
nowhere on earth can you visit
the land of Negro
if you search earth's entire span

Now digest please this trivia
Bolivians come from Bolivia
and Japanese they come from Japan
Austrians come from Austria
Australians from Australia
and I declare, Egyptians
they come from Egypt land

Check it; from the instant of your birth
you can search this entire earth
and believe this, no matter how far you go
No matter what the latitude
the most determined attitude
will never find a land called Negro

You see Negro is a name
put on us to bring shame
and separate us from our Ancestral Mother
cut our ties to our vast estate
cause a self-destructive hate
and stop us from caring for one another

But Hatred, you shall lose
cause we Africans in America choose
to love ourselves, we thought you'd like to know
and now that we're awake
whatever trips we take
won't come near your mythical land, called Negro

There's no such people, no such place
and we should never disgrace
the spirit of our Ancestors again
by answering to the call
of a name that brought us all
pain after pain, after pain...

We are not Negroes, N-Words
nor anything else absurd

Negrosity

I had the pleasure one day,
a blessing I'd say,
of conversing with Amiri Baraka.
He explained to me,
in words I could see,
some truths that would plainly shock ya.

This one thing he said,
stands out in my head,
that especially peaked my curiosity.
He used a term,
that made me squirm,
I refer here to "Negrosity."

He said, "Most of our folk,
are fastened with a yoke,
tethered by restraints not seen.
There are shackles on our brains,
our mentality's in chains,
hooked on social amphetamines.

We are perpetual consumers,
food for parasitic tumors,
that devour and thrive off our labor.
Negrosity is the condition,
that hinders our fruition,
we must quit this foolish behavior."

"So, what good sir,
would you prefer,
we do to correct this hideosity?
What steps may be taken,
now that we've awakened,
from this sleep called Negrosity?"

"A good question son,
is always one,
where the answer lies deep inside,

if you take inventory,
on yours and his-story,
the solution is spiritual race pride."

"Whoa now, the mere mention of race,
brings a frown to one's face,
and most times elicits animosity,
and how can spirit solve,
what the race has evolved,
and what's pride got to do with Negrosity?"
"Taking pride in your race,
will incite you to trace,
your ancestor's magnificent luminosity,
then you'll find categorically,
no question historically,
we're victims of semiotic atrocities.

There are no Negroes you see,
and Negrosity,
is not even really a word,
And the fact that we answer,
to this semantic cancer,
makes it all the more absurd.

Being proud of who you are,
will diminish the scar,
left by generations of deception.
Spiritual pride in oneself,
will restore your health,
to this rule, there can be no exception.

So its time you paid yourself,
And enjoyed the world's wealth,
God knows you've been full of generosity.
And remove the stigma,
that caused this enigma.
Take off the shackle of Negrosity!"

June 1999, Result of a conversation with Amiri Baraka

When

If you actually realized you were committing a sin,
at what point exactly would you stop it, my friend?
If it dawned on you suddenly you were
wasting your time,
When would you do something, When; it's your prime?

If it suddenly hit you, something inside,
that you were lacking an ingredient,
lacking race pride?

If you knew the word Negro was causing you pain,
would you continue to use it, again and again?

When would you stop clinging to a slave-master's trick?
When; when you're absolutely sure there's
no more cotton to pick.
When will you stop teaching your children the same,
sinful disobedience that has always brought shame?
When will you start using your free national name?

And when will you understand that
the last train down the track,

is the one carrying those people referred to as black?
When will you stop using the word nigger so often,
When your mouth is sealed by the lid of a coffin?

When, brothers and sisters, when will come that day,
when we take the marks of slavery
and throw them away?

And finally take our places in the affairs of men,
I wonder, my brothers and sisters, I wonder, when?

September 1983

My 40 Acres & My Mule

There are some issues need addressing
some sins that need confessing
Truth is I've been used like a tool
for all these years I've worked
yet I'm still being jerked
Where are my 40 acres and my mule

The Pope confessed his dirt
to the millions the Vatican hurt
to the Jews who lost their lives in the holocaust
but not once has he mentioned
its slave-trading dimension
or the 100 million African souls lost

Tell me how long will these nations
continue their starvation
of those on whose backs they were built
How long will white lies
flourish while a black dies
Tell me, how much more blood must be spilt

I'm tired of playing the fool
What happened to the golden rule
Tell me, where are my 40 acres and my mule
Where's my 40 acres and my mule?

April 2000

Commentary on Muhammad Ali

"Service to others is the rent you pay for your room here on earth."

-Muhammad Ali, *Time Magazine* (1978)

Muhammad Ali deserves a whole chapter in this book because he represents a whole chapter in my life. Like countless others, I was influenced by the sheer magnitude of the man. He was the definition of pride in the hearts and minds of African people all over the world. When James Brown sang "Say It loud, I'm black and I'm proud," the image that always came to my mind was Muhammad Ali. Nobody could beat the Champ, not even when Joe Frazier won in Madison Square Garden was Ali ever defeated in the eyes of the African Diaspora. He still reigned in the minds of the people, because of what he stood for. When we consider what he sacrificed for his honor and beliefs, you can't help but marvel at the sheer strength of his character.

We all understood that most of his boasting was showmanship. In our hearts, we knew he was acting. Yet, in the back of our minds, we knew he wasn't jiving either. This dude could do everything he said. We cannot underestimate the volume, the extent, or the degree to which he changed the psyche of both black and white people in this country. He certainly changed my entire perception of myself. He single-handedly raised my level of self-esteem. I can remember physically tilting my chin higher at the mere mention of his name. He is a true giant among men.

When one thinks of David slaying Goliath, what occurred between Ali and the U. S. Government concerning the draft takes on almost biblical proportions. When he took his stand and made the decision not to serve in Vietnam, he shook up the world. I can count at least 10 brothers from my neighborhood alone that died as a result of those senseless acts of American aggression and imperialism. He expressed my sentiments exactly when he said he would not go kill Vietnamese people who had never done any harm to him just because the government
said so. Muhammad was speaking for me and I would rather have died for him and our mutual belief than gone off and murdered people who were never my enemy.

God knows, I loved that man and still love him. He gave us a sense of worth in a time when we found little within ourselves worthy. He forced us to appreciate our own greatness by forcing us to focus on his. He was and is my hero and perhaps the greatest internationally acclaimed role model for black men that America has ever seen. He demonstrated to us that we are the greatest. We stood on his shoulders and he never wavered. When he rumbled, not once did he stumble, not once did he fall. Today, in the year 2010, he is still the "Greatest of All Time."

"I know I got it made while the masses of black people are catchin' hell, but as long as they ain't free, I ain't free."

- Muhammad Ali, *Playboy Magazine* (1975)

Thank You Muhammad Ali

Every single time that we
questioned our mortality
the strongest image we could see
was that of you, Muhammad Ali

You made our spirits grow
When racism said we couldn't
self-doubt said we shouldn't
and self-esteem was at an all time low
You gave us back our pride
put courage back inside
We love you and want you to know

The way you stood up for yourself
gave our whole race wealth
wealth that comes only from the heart
The way you danced around the ring
made our proud hearts sing
and we loved you from the very start

Your extremely handsome face
delighted our whole race
and when you spoke we all just had to smile
with every word you said
we would elevate our heads
and gloat for just a little while

When you said you would not kill
for someone else's thrill
Would not war against those not your enemy
You shook up the world
You precious African pearl
and we'll love you straight through infinity

The strength in your resolve
helped us all solve
problems in our everyday existence
You shouted long and loud
stood up straight and proud
and we flew on the wings of your persistence

Again, thank you Muhammad
for we are truly honored
to have you in our hearts and minds
It was you who said it best
Your words still stand the test
"You are the Greatest of All Time!"

"I am America. I am the part you won't recognize. But get used to me. Black, confident, cocky; my name, not yours; my religion, not yours; my goals, my own; get used to me."

-Muhammad Ali – *The Greatest* (1975)

Where I Came From

Where I came from, we weren't absolutely certain we
would eat every day...
Sometimes roaches would ascend and descend up and
down the radiator pipe into Miss Jenkin's house…
Ma said the roaches came from Miss Jenkin's house
'cause she was nasty...

Where I came from, grass was something we saw on the
high school football field... Grass…

Where I came from, if the liquor stores, located on every
corner, were closed; you could always run down to Mr.
Jack's joint and get you a half-pint...

Where I came from, first base was Miss Betty's Buick,
second base was the lamp post, third was the fire
hydrant, if the cars weren't comin', and home plate was
the same cement square you played hop scotch in when
you weren't playin' stick ball...

Where I came from Pookey was accepted, he
would get drunk and pass out right on our tenement
steps and all we would do is suck our teeth and step
over him...

And Mr. James, Mr. James was a genius; he could book
the numbers without paper or pencil—genius…
Where I came from, courage and valor were equated
with insanity, "don't mess with Smoke, he crazy. He
already killed two people." He crazy...

Where I came from, flowers bloomed in the pots of very
few folk's windows...

Where I came from was like a jungle, and sometimes I
do wonder, how I kept from goin' under…

Where I came from, jail was like a right-of-passage…
"You seen Junebug, he lookin' good ain't he? You know
he just came home…"

Where I came from we'd mostly hide from the truth,
behind the tinted glass of a whisky bottle
or in the contents of a hypodermic syringe...

Where I came from, women weren't respectin' us men
much, 'cause somehow, for some reason; we weren't
respectin' ourselves…
"Girl, if the government catches that man in your house,
they gonna cut your check off..."
"What's more important, the money or the man?" "Girl
you betta get that check…"

Where I came from, most of the men had lost their
ambition somewhere and the majority never found it…
As a matter of fact, where I came from, the women were
raisin' the boys…
Most of the men were beaten or broken or gone...

Where I came from education was secondary to survival,
or maybe thirdary or maybe even fourthdary…
Where I came from drug dealin' was socially accepted,
'cause some people misinterpreted the phrase, "by any
means necessary..."

Sometimes I wonder if it's my fault,
where I came from…
Some times I wonder, if I came from somewhere else,
would I be as strong as I am today?
"Do you know where I'm comin' from?"

Where Were You Dad?
(A Penitentiary Saga)

Where were you Dad
Perhaps you should know
that had you been there
to help me grow

I never would have stuck
that needle in my arm
and that bank teller
I would not have harmed

Cause had you taught me
to LOVE instead of hate
I'd be doing interviews
instead of life plus 38

If I'd been taught OBEDIENCE
I would have blessed you
rather than all those crimes
I finally confessed to

The world would've benefited
had I been taught GRATITUDE
instead of this bitter man
with this angry assed attitude

Had I been taught MODESTY
your name would not be defamed
for all the crimes I committed
I would not now be ashamed

Cause had you taught me CHARITY
I would have gained love
instead of languishing in this cell
with a bunk-bed above

Had I been taught TEMPERANCE
my temper never would have flared
Just where were you Dad
When I was young, frightened & scared

Had I been taught PRUDENCE
my fortune would've been good
instead I wreaked havoc
throughout my neighborhood

Had you taught me JUSTICE
I'd have been honored by the world
instead I'm pressing iron
and doing bicep curls

Had I been taught SINCERITY
my heart would not reproach me
instead of this dismal crypt
where evil approaches me

Had you taught me DILIGENCE
my wealth would have increased
instead of this eight by eight
where my spirit is deceased

Had you taught me BENEVOLENCE
my mind would've been exalted
instead of this penal warehouse
where all decency has defaulted

Had you taught me SCIENCE
my life would have been useful
instead of turning out to be
this sorry excuse for…A man

And had you taught me SPIRITUALITY
at least my death would be happy
but alas, you even deprived me of that...
Where were you Dad?

October 1980

One Degree of Separation

There's a problem in our communities
and someone must step to the plate
Cause there's a whole population
that could credit this nation
We must R.E.A.C.H. them before it's too late

We are labeled "Ex-Offenders"
labeled "At-Risk Youth"
but what separates you from me
It's a simple opportunity
We must come to grips with this truth

Cause America's founding fathers
were fathered by ex-offenders
and the record reflects
we are all suspects
we're a nation of great pretenders

So this may cause some trepidation
and you might not like this observation
but between you and me
there's only one degree
just one degree of separation

January 2003, Written for the R.E.A.C.H. organization

Opportunity

I gazed at OPPORTUNITY
As she walked into the place
But instead of me embracing her
I laughed right in her face

Nevertheless she flirted
In spite of my naiveté
She said "soon you'll learn to love me
And come to bless this day"

But alas, I was a youngster
All brash and full of self
I chose to throw her jewels
In the closet on a shelf

I shut the door behind me
Walked away from fortune good
And chose to dance with chance
Whom I never understood

But OPPORTUNITY is patient
As tolerant as can be
And neither she nor my Creator
Were yet quite through with me

So She, along with Destiny
Came a knocking yet once more
This time I was elated
To see her standing at my door

And I guess if there's a moral
Somewhere lurking round this rhyme
It's that if when first you meet her
You should hug her that first time

But if at first you fail
Pursuing OPPORTUNITY
Remember she's a lady
And the lady catches thee

opportunity

Anatomy of the 7

Consider the 7 for one second
maybe 7 seconds or more
7 is a number
one could truly adore

Over 7 sacred hills
we all must travel
before strict Father Time
drops His coming home gavel

7 seas, 7 continents
7 wonders of the world
7 layers of skin on
every beautiful girl

Yeah, 7 is the symbol
of perfection you see
There 7 layers of bark
on every full-grown tree

There are 7 glorious colors
in the prismatic scheme
Then there's that 7-year itch
You know what I mean

Atmosphere, stratosphere
yeah, they're 7 of those
7 holes in your head
counting the 2 in your nose

They're 7 whole notes
on the musical scale
7 fathoms to the ocean
where swims the whale

7 days in creation
where all was manifested
worked 6 days that week
on the 7th He rested

They say the 7th sign
signals the end
So think before committing
that 7th deadly sin

Consider your deeds
at least 7 times 7
You might wind up
in that 7th heaven
07/07/07 Seriously…

12 Rounds to Victory

In life we must all be fighters
determined not to go down
'cause the ref only raises
the glove of the bravest
the strongest after 12 rounds

The first round may throw you some jabs
some hooks and crosses not seen
Some stiff uppercuts
that punish your gut
'cause life can be vicious and mean

The second and third may be tricky
your rival, better than you thought
After four and five
not sure you'll survive,
questioning the skills that you brought

But the heart of a champion is in you
placed there by God, most wise
through six, seven and eight
you demonstrate
why the toughest get the prize

Through nine you may be quite weary
battered and bruised through round ten
Here is where you start
to reach in your heart
and pull out that second wind

By eleven you see your opponent
is beaten and broken down
You smile 'cause your skill
and indomitable will
leaves you standing after 12 rounds

You're the victor after 12 rounds
January 2001, for my friend Roger Leonard

A Wedding Prayer

Today we take these wedding vows
we promise each other to cherish
and pray our Lord is watching now
to insure this bond won't perish

Today our love flames burn
our passion warm and glowing
We pray as the seasons turn
Love and Respect keep growing

Today sweet promises we make
as we link our souls together
We pray this bond never breaks
and last till the twelfth of forever

Today we walk this isle
in sweet anticipation
and pray our heartfelt smiles
remain through generations

Today we wish and hope
this wedding prayer is heard
God bless this wonderful day
and our dreams be not deferred
Amen

Marriage Instructions

When the stress of each day
seems to get in the way
and you can hardly stand one another
remember this minute
and all the joy in it
and the love you feel for each other

When problems arise
and Satan tries
to destroy this spiritual union
Find strength in your soul
and God will unfold
his reasons for this communion

Be faithful to your bed
there'll be no tears shed
and there'll be pleasure under your roof
Faithfulness to your spouse
will keep joy in your house
your happiness shall be the proof

Constantly look,
at the vows you took,
and patience must be your eyes.
Search for each other's good,
as you said you would,
and Peace will be your prize.

At last, keep all faults,
locked in sealed vaults,
and never look down your nose.
Then you'll remain friends,
till the world ends,
That's it, you win, case closed.

June 1998, instructions for a happy couple

Big Chair Chess Club

This is the story of a chess club
founded for inner city youth.
Yet it's different from most,
it's distinguished and boasts,
of teaching not just chess, but truth.

It teaches young people to reason,
to deduce and to rationalize.
Use logic and intelligence,
cast a positive spell against,
deception, treachery and lies.

'Cause Chess is the game of the Regal,
and Big Chair teaches just that.
Our ancestors were noble,
and their influence global,
our history reflects these facts.

So at Big Chair we're on a mission,
to the minds of our children improve,
and teach the un-teachable,
reach the un-reachable,
and always think before you move.

September 2003, for Eugene Brown and the Big Chair Chess Club

Cloud Song

I wished upon a cloud one day
and asked its beauty
what it would say
If it had voice
and song, like me
while floating high
above so free
What message
would it sing to me

If I could sing the
cloud said proud
I would not sing
so very loud
I'd whisper soft
sweet melodies
like those you hear
in wind swept trees

My song would calm
the restless soul
and warm the hearts
of those turned cold
From where I rest
above all things
I'd sing of all
that good cheer brings

For as I gaze
from my lofty view
I see the miracle
in each of you
Because I see things
from high above
my song would be
a song of love

But since our Maker
has not allowed
music to rain down
from this cloud
I trust in you
my dear friend
to sing my song
and make it end

on a high note
sweet and clear
because I feel your harmony
way up here…

Heal a Parent–Heal a Child

Want to end neighborhood violence
so peace may preside for a while
Then forgo your vow of silence
speak to a parent, speak to a child

You say there's too much drug use
and your neighborhood's defiled
Then why not try some hug use
Hug a parent, Hug a child

It is said, "it takes a village"
and that proverb makes me smile
we're going to need some courage
to engage that parent and that child

Because hurt people, hurt people
regarding this there's no denial
You want to heal your neighborhood
Heal a parent, heal a child

August 2003, for Theme Poem for DMH DC CINGS
Social
Marketing Campaign

History of the Ad

The first commercial written
caused an apple to be bitten
poor Adam, smitten; influenced by Eve
The serpent's smooth enticement
was a nicely done advertisement
Its long range impact brilliantly conceived

For he knew their purchasing power
would increase with each hour
and eventually, Eve would find the mall
Her nakedness loathing
she must buy proper clothing
must catch that summer sale, before the fall

Aged Methuselah, plugged Viagra
and sales flowed like the Niagara
he married at age one hundred eleven
The poster boy for virility
put a freeze frame on senility
his first son born at age one eighty seven

Old Noah in the Eden Gazette
placed an ad that ended up wet
as the copy called for lots of rain
He advertised that water
would soon flood every quarter
but alas, no one paid heed to his campaign

King Solomon built the temple
but the task was not that simple
he wanted a campaign with pomp and poise
He needed architects and masons
to lay a sure foundation
and do it without making any noise

Back in Sodom and Gomorrah
it's related in the Torah
Old Lot beseeched his wife not to fault
But she promptly fell victim
to a very slick ad dictum
that turned her head, and changed her flesh to salt

And at Delilah's cut and curl
strong Samson's favorite girl
had coupons reading bearer gets half off
But little did he know
his strength would up and go
the instant he let her cut his hair off

Yes, the ad has been around
for as long as there's been sound
and believe this, the ad is here to stay
Two questions then ring true
first, may we create one for you
and, how much are willing to pay

February 2000, written for an advertising agency
campaign contest

Plump

They called me plump and chubby
big boned and heavy set
said your momma is fat
and your daddy's like that
you'll be too; I'm willing to bet

So I lived to their expectations
and I ate whatever was near
till my gut overflowed
to the next zip-code
while my heart pulsated in fear

My pride and esteem deflated
truth is, I despised myself
Detested all mirrors
was always in fear of
prognosis of failing health

My blood vessels they contorted
doctor's whispered Diabetes
and the stress of its mention
caused more hypertension
since I dreaded the feared disease

And that STRESS, oh it's a monster
cause your mind will make it worse
As you dig your own grave
by the way you behave
living up to the hater's curse
of Plump…

Wanted

She was brown…
Not your mediocre brown…
But a luscious dark delicious…
Hershey un-commercialized brown…
A chocolate dream…
Deep, creamy and unblemished…
She radiated smooth…
Emitted majesty…
Regal oozed out of her pores…
Her confidence wafted across continents…
Her intelligence was absolutely intoxicating…
And the moment I saw her I knew…
Black she was…
African she was…
Angel she was…
Queen she was…
Woman she was…
She was...
All…
I ever…
Wanted

Melanin, Sweet Melanin

Let's talk a few minutes about melanin
Consider some things if you would
Let's try to get up under our skin
They're some things if you don't know, you should

Melanin you see is the primary cause
its the balm that makes us so smooth
Without it some folk break spiritual laws
Its absence makes some folk uncouth

Without it your brain would completely shut down
No rhythm no rhyme no dance
without black melanin you couldn't hear a sound
and your eyes would never glance

At the base of your brain is the Locus Ceruleus*
where sweet black melanin's contained
And the God of our Fathers put plenty in us
but with others, He refrained

Your melanin is more than just pigment you know
your melanin controls your psyche
It's a gift your Creator saw fit to bestow
and why Mike flew so high in those Nikes

It's why we jump higher; it's why we run faster
It's why we wrinkle less too
It's why we love stronger
It's why we pray longer
And why we forgive and bless you

Melanin enhances
all circumstances
It's why we are so spiritual
the lack of it lances
makes evil advances
thinks linear, seldom spherical

And the blacker the berry the sweeter the juice
All crave tall, dark and handsome
It's how we survived such physical abuse
and why we've been held for ransom

So let nobody fool you
I'm here to school you
Your melanin is an asset
And many are they
Who if had their way
Would sit exactly where your assets

So cherish your blessing
start right now confessing
your love, for your built-in tan
And thank God again
for the skin that you're in
Give Him all the praise that you can

Give Him all the praise you can…

"When I found I had crossed that line, /on her first escape from slavery, 1845/ *I looked at my hands to see if I was the same person. There was such a glory over everything."*
-Harriet Tubman (1868)

* Locus Ceruleus:
http://en.wikipedia.org/wiki/Locus_ceruleus

Sole/Soul Sista

Yes you are my soul sista…
Greatest story ever told sista…
You're my whole sista…
Strong and in control sista…
Powerful, forceful, bold sista…
Warm me when I'm cold sista…
Cook that casserole sista…
Yes you are my sole sista…
Creator broke the mold sista…
After you the tale's retold sista…
In you I unfold sista…
You're my light beyond the pole sista…
Got that hidden sexy mole sista…
I'll spend my whole bankroll sista…
I'm weak when you cajole sista…
And since we took that stroll sista…
I've grown a thousand fold sista….
For this you must be told sista…
I'll die to you uphold sista…
Your dignity's unsold sista…
With skin like dark spun gold sista…
And eyes like deep charcoal sista…
Again, He broke the mold sista…
Lord, you just ice cold sista…
The prophets they foretold sista…

Of your talents manifold sista…
You manage our household sista…
Protecting your stronghold sista…

With wit sometimes you scold sista…
Make me crawl in a wormhole sista…
You take no rigmarole sista…
At times you just so bold sista…
Your demeanor takes its toll sista…
Then you open that sugar bowl sista…
Make me buy that mink stole sista…
Again, you in control sista…
Yes you are my sole/soul sista…
And I wouldn't have it any other way…

Angela Davis

Opinion on: Stress

Who am I? And how do I qualify to conduct workshops on stress?

I conduct stress management seminars for a living and am certified as a stress management therapist through the National Association of Drug and Alcohol Interventionists. I was asked the above question by a blue-nosed intellectual in a room full of PhD's at the DC Department of Mental health. And I thought my response might interest you and serve the overall purpose of this book. Here was my poetic response.

"I have the royal blood of Akhenaton coursing through my veins and the intellect of Imhotep conceptualizing my brain. I am the father of medicine as we know it and gave Hiram Abiff the architectural renderings that allowed him to construct King Solomon's Temple without making any noise. Yet I find myself here in America at the bottom of the intellectual totem pole.

I once socialized with Ramses and King Tutankhamen, had high tea with Cleopatra and Cheop, yet I find myself on the lowest rungs of America's social ladders. I swapped esoteric jokes with Amen Ra, Abraham, Moses, Buddha, Muhammad and Jesus, then taught the Greeks the meaning of spirituality yet I find myself here in America caught up in a religious twilight zone. It was me who first glimpsed the dawn of civilization when some men were groping in the dark, afraid of fire and thought the world was flat. Yet I find myself being called savage and subjugated by the very same people I helped to civilize.

I look around and see America the beautiful, with her amber waves of grain that I planted. I see purple mountains of majesty above fruited planes that I harvested. From sea to shinning sea, I see that God has shed His grace on thee America...but America seems to have forgotten me. Maybe not to you but to me, this is extremely stressful.

The same information I gave to Khufu/Cheop at Giza, on how to construct all of the roads that lead to the Great Pyramid, I gave to the Army Corp of Engineers here on how to lay out the most elaborate and efficient systems of roadways in the civilized world. Yet I find myself terrorized every time I take to the very roads I built with my blood, sweat and tears...terrorized because of the undeclared crime of 'driving while black.' It was me who laid the architectural framework for the nation's capital yet I find myself being gentrified right out of the very houses I built. I have a hard time crossing bridges; as a matter of fact I sometimes hyperventilate approaching tall bridges. Not because I'm afraid of heights but because I get knots in my stomach thinking about how many slaves lost their lives laying those bridge foundation stones.

I get stressed thinking about how far my people are behind educationally, knowing that being denied education is the reason why we're so far behind. I get stressed thinking about how all of my customs, culture and traditions were stripped from me and that I don't even know my real name. I have been at war and suffering from Post Traumatic Stress Disorder since 1619 when I came in chains. I've been at war with myself and my captors since Willie Lynch outlined the blueprint for my exploitation at Jamestown, Virginia.

I'm a psychological, sociological, educational and financial wreck. My gut tells me something is wrong when the overwhelming majority of the more than 2 million people locked away in prison cells for crimes against themselves look just like me. Hypertension, high blood pressure, stroke and ultimate heart failure sits on my doorstep and dares me to come out and play. I have stomach acid churning and turning with rumblings and grumblings of gastrointestinal cravings for Tums, Rolaids and Pepcid AC every time I remember that my ancestors labor wont even buy me health care in my country.

Do I qualify to conduct workshops on stress? Please allow me to answer by first asking, does your theory qualify you more than my experience?" And second, after surviving all the above, if I don't qualify then who does?"

Needless to say, I got the job.

Dear reader, I consider stress to be the number one problem facing African Americans today. Stress is a disease. As a matter of fact stress *is* dis-ease, literally. Stress has been defined by Dr. Hans Selye as a 'nonspecific response of the body to any demand.' It has been described, not so much as a thing, but a condition of the mind that reflects its symptoms in the body. More than 20 years ago researchers at Cornell University Medical College reported that, "stress is the most debilitating medical and social problem in the United States today." That was before we had 24 hour cable news channels, satellite radio, personal computers, fax machines, pagers, palm pilots and cell phones. That was before daily-televised war and September eleventh, with its yellow, orange and red terror alerts. What the Black Plague was to Europe in the Dark Ages, stress is to America in this electronic age.

Stress is ubiquitous. It permeates throughout our society. It is evident in short fuses and quick tempers played out in road rage and school shootings. According to the U.S. Justice Department there is a crime of violence committed every four seconds in this country. It is eating at the very fabric of this society. Since 2000 there have been more over 2 million incidences of violence in the workplace annually according to the U.S. Department of Labor. In 2005 there were more than 4 million reported domestic violence cases and America's murder rate outnumbered the entire populations of many small countries.

Stress-related child abuse and spousal abuse are at their highest levels in the history of mankind. Stress-related substance abuse is drugging the heart of America. Consider that we consume 75 to 85% of all the cocaine manufactured in the entire world. In the year 2002 Americans consumed more than 6 billion tranquilizers. Dear reader; that is enough dope to sedate everybody on the planet. The National Institute of Drug Abuse (NIDA) recently reported that as a country America represents approximately 5% of the world's population, yet we consume more than 60% of the world's drugs. The suicide rate among our babies 8 to 12 years old has risen by more than 100% in the last decade. The third leading cause of death among young people 14 to 24 years old is suicide and according to data released by the National Institute of Mental Health, there is a successful suicide every 17 minutes in the U.S. with a serious but failed attempt every single minute. Consider just how drastic that is. That means that if it took you 51 minutes to read half of this book that by the time you did so, statistically 3 people will have taken their own lives and 51 people will have made a serious attempt. Houston, we have identified the problem. Stress!!!

It's rather mind-boggling that stress could be such a vicious culprit responsible for so many maladies. When we normally think of disease, we think of AIDS, Tuberculosis, Cancer or some viral infection that we can see through a microscope or view on an x-ray screen. But stress is different from what we commonly consider a disease. It is woven into the fabric of our lives. It's not a germ we can identify in a Petri-dish or see swimming down the streams of our blood. It is much more diabolical than that. Stress is a slick disease, a slimy, slithering, sleazy slough of poisoned ideas that lurk in dark shadows behind emotions and attitudes. Stress prowls around our minds and bodies and is equally the cause and effect of how the mind and body function and interact. Stress is literally psychosomatic; *Psycho*, meaning mind/mental and *Soma*, meaning body/physical.

Stress is the result of how we have unconsciously and consciously made the decision to live our lives. It is the illness created by abusing our minds and bodies, which lead up to a myriad of negative symptoms. They range from losing it in the car, (road rage) a temper tantrum, to full-blown heart attack and death. The symptoms are legion, from overeating and alcoholism to insomnia and loss of libido. Stress can cause nervous ticks and stomach ulcers, hyperventilation and acne. It causes stomach acid to churn creating acid reflux. Stress has driven people from drug-addicted depression to self-mutilation. It has been called the silent killer. According to Dr. Phil Nuernberger, in his book, *Freedom from Stress - a Holistic Approach*, "stress is more than being uptight occasionally, or having a bad day. It is a recurring imbalance resulting in the daily wear-and-tear on the body that leads to dysfunction and debilitation."

Now being black in America and suffering from Post Traumatic Slavery/Stress Syndrome, people need to know that stress has taken up permanent residence and travels with us. So much so that it has wrapped itself around the double helix in the DNA of all the offspring of slaves in this country.

Consider; DNA is described as *various nucleic acids that are the molecular basis of heredity.* If this is so, then we have inherited more than 300 years of the worst sustained stressful oppression inflicted on human beings in the history of mankind.

Stress Test

This morning a siren woke me
and it caused my head to ache
Its long wailing cries
yanked the sleep from my eyes
Which one of these pills should I take

Then I turn on the news while preparing
to drive to this job that I hate
But it's so depressing
I can't help from stressing
plus I'm already one hour late

Next, my car, when I started it coughed
then trembled as if it were ill
And I knew that this day
would be hell to pay
I just hope I took the right pill

Now the lady ahead has her neck craned
cause her make-up's not layered quite right
And while her mirrors abused
I'm all confused
'cause the driver behind wants to fight

Then the beltway, it got me all nervous
just trying to get off the on ramp
'cause want-a-be Andretti
and could-a-been Kyle Petty
say the speed limit must be revamped

Now I spend the next hour and one half
midst fools playing car lane hopscotch
Between truck horns blaring
and maniacs swearing
my stress has been turned up a notch

So I say prayers as I step from my car
asking heaven to help with this mess
Dear God I pray
help me get through this day
Lord, help me pass this stress test

Slam Your Stress

Slamming Your Stress
puts fears to rest
It heightens your self-esteem
Your soul expressed
yourself you bless
you learn to live your dreams

February 2000

Valley of Despair

Beware good people, beware the valley of despair
a place we all visit but none should dwell there

A place where we give serious thought
to all of the lessons misery taught

Where the racked with disease, the sick and the lame
find reason after reason, for themselves to blame

Despair is the land where entering its gate
you find the hopeless, the lame and the pitiful wait

Where not a gleam of joy is in any eye
where weepers and wailers lay around and cry

If you came to party you have no chance
'cause fear and dread won't allow you to dance

Only lovers of weeping are allowed to play
If you have any hope you cannot stay

Yet we find ourselves there wallowing in dirt
unconscious of the fact that we caused the hurt

If you would avoid what hurts you the most
don't bring pain to the party, remember you're the host

Leave this Valley of Despair where misery is king
the valley in the shadow of depression's wing

And please, if you're visiting, get out today
just over the next rise, there's a much better way

June 1979, Lexington, Kentucky

The Flood

Take heed folks, seriously
that this verse be understood
you're about to hear a lesson
taught for your own good

You see there were some folk in Noah's day
who thought the man a fool,
they'd laugh and mock and point and scorn
and viciously ridicule

Why "Noah, they'd say, 'have you lost your wit?
There are no clouds in sight,
Do you expect us to worry about rain,
while there's fun to be had tonight?"

"Evidently my Brother
there is a problem in your mind,
for you labor to build a ship
where there is no water to find."

And because of their disbelief
found themselves stuck in waste high mud
until that awful hour
when they were drowned by the flood

Now the "Word" has come once more
the same as it did then
with a warning for the people
a warning once again

And our Temple, like the Ark
has its doors wide open
and it's on us to heed the "Word"
the Prophet's have spoken

Now Noah lost a home
and some friends to the floodtide
and those who swam up late
knocked, but couldn't get inside

So we should learn a lesson
from the one those people taught
outside the Arc's doors
we don't want to be caught

And we should praise the Father
for granting us a space
inside His many Mansions
a safe and warm place

The Test

When there is trouble in the land
and you must take a stand
keep hope and faith at the ready
for you must bear in mind,
that with the passage of time
ill winds make the strong steady

Even in the midst of war
be faithful to the core
and forsake not your aim
for the goal you're seeking
you should be peaking
at just about the end of the game

When the road's really rough
the night cold and tough
and ahead seems all dark and drear
make your faith grow stronger
hold on a little longer
in a minute things cloudy come clear

Through the worst the wise
keep their eye on the prize
and always find means of good
keep their faith and obey
believe not in doomsday
and strive to be the best they could

So press on regardless
and you will find the hardest
was really a simple little test
and the effort you put in it
was the proof that you would win it
and the Test was really for the best

May 1981, after a toothache in Lexington Kentucky

Thanks Oprah

Oprah beloved…Oprah you visit me
in a place not lit by common light you see
You come and touch my feelings inside
You give my spirit a sweet joy ride
You calm the restless troubled soul
You warm the hearts of those turned cold
You rescue stranded, tattered lives
mending broken husbands
restoring battered wives
An angel you are
on a mission
sharing, loving
unconditioned
The more I watch you
the more I see
I love you, beloved Oprah
for visiting me
Thank you sincerely…

You Special

I member when you didn't have no real shoes...
Now you actin' like you special, cause you got enough
money to buy you a coat with somebody else's
name on it...
Please...
Member when you had to borrow the mayonnaise
for a mayonnaise samich?

You member that time that roach crawled out the back of
your shirt collar, in school?
I remember.
But now…you special...

You better than folks, tiltin' your head back,
lookin' down your nose, like you special...

Member when you chased the bus half way down the
block, so I could throw you my transfer out the window?
Member?

Member beggin' for nickels and dimes
so we could get us a pint
of Wild Irish Rose and a pack of Kools?

Member that time you made that big jar of red Kool-Aid
and stuck it in the frigerator while you knocked on four
different peoples' doors, tryin' to borrow some sugar to
sweeten it?
You member that time your step-father got drunk and
hit you so hard, your head knocked a hole in the wall in
your livin' room, and the next day yawl put the little TV
in front of it? Remember?

But now… now you can afford
to buy you some sneakers
with a swoosh on it, you special...

Redeem the Dream

Now this poetic statement
may seem to some extreme
Yet a people climb no higher
than the summit of their dreams

So we must plan this hour
an elaborate spiritual scheme
For the sake of all humanity
we must redeem the dream

Cause if the Reverend Doctor
were standing here today
I'm not sure that he'd be pleased
not certain what he'd say

It's been more than 40 years
since that faith-filled day
Still the circumstances
have not gone away

Because police brutality
cast a shadow on our dreams
A blue haze prevents the raising
of our people's self esteem

America must realize
Its folk are under attack
The victims being assaulted
are those driving while black

Some men in blue we've chosen
to protect and serve
seize every opportunity
to kick us to the curb

Of the 2 million Americans
locked up in our jails

8 out of 10 is a black man
How did Justice tip the scales

I thought Justice was blindfolded
She must be reading Braille
Obviously she's not colorblind
she obviously favors pale

This poem is a plea for justice
to right this grievous wrong
It's time the burden was lifted
we carried the load too long

From all the melanised people
oppressed by men in blue
this poem is a prayerful out-cry
that we are human too

In the name of God, we ask
Call off your cruel regime
In the name of God, we pray
Dear Lord, redeem the dream

Your True Worth

Using the U.S. Constitution
our African contributions
were the roads on which your prosperity was paved
See the 13th amendment clause
says the breaking of certain laws
makes it all right to manufacture slaves

So you sit in your boardroom
and design the black man's doom
shipping heroin, crack and guns to our neighborhood
with clever, covert instructions
for these weapons of mass destruction
to suppress and lock us up for good

And once jailed in your institutions
we're forced into false-restitution
While working for slave labor wages
and that's 21st Century slavery
While you lie, and call yours bravery
So who really should be locked up in your cages

But your weapons of mass destruction
I declare, shall be your induction
to the hell you make for others on earth
and your offspring shall burn by the fire
of your greed and selfish desire
then the world shall know your true worth

Yes…the world will know your true worth

"As long as the colored man look to white folks to put the crown on what he say . . . as long as he looks to white folks for approval . . . then he ain't never gonna find out who he is and what he's about."
-August Wilson, *Ma Rainey's Black Bottom,* Act 1 (1984)

Seven Little Boys

Last night my son had a sleepover
There were six little boys, plus me
The seven of us
formed a bond of trust
A pleasure and a joy to see

They laughed at a world still funny
untainted by life's toxicities
We wrestled and played
their nerves un-frayed
with no thoughts of life's complexities

How simple life seems at eleven
How near seem life's simple joys
Last night I re-kindled
a flame that had dwindled
Last night, we were seven little boys

10 March 2002

Sirens & Police Badges

Sirens wail screaming to a decibel deafening
round my way...

Police badges flash behind my eye-sockets
like July 4th fireworks...

I should celebrate the sound...
I should welcome the sight…
Instead, I lament the noise
and squeeze my eyelids shut…

As they take my mommy and daddy away…
For pursuing the dream…
Just as they were instructed…

I'm scared to death of sirens & police badges...

August 1969
It ain't changed and this is 2010…

Watch

Where are the children heading?
A good question we should ask.
Where are the children heading?
We should take that question to task.

Where are our young folk going?
Are we truly concerned?
Or is our primary interest,
how much money we have earned?

Where are the children heading?
Watch, and it can be seen,
a spiritual ingredient is missing.
Some are angry, some are mean.

Where are our children heading?
Why, only where we lead.
Wonder what's more important,
their welfare, or our greed?

If we want to stop the violence,
and bring peace back in the schools,
we have to talk *"to"* our children,
not *"at"* them like they're fools.

"We" have to stop the violence,
in the media, that's all they're fed.
Our children are not the problem,
our children are being misled.

We have to bring the spirit,
of LOVE back in the class.
That's the only way our children,
are ever going to pass.

If we teach TRUTH up in that classroom,
and turn LOVE up a notch,
we needn't worry where they're heading,
all we have to do is WATCH.

June 1995, for Jo Patterson and the Parent Watch organization

The Mighty Pen

The pen is mighty
stronger than steel
can make or break
has mass appeal

Ask a native
born in this land
What the pen can do
in the devil's hand

Or Nelson Mandela
who for 27 years
because of a pen
shed incarcerated tears

Old Henry Hudson
purchased all of Manhattan
with some beads, some trinkets
and a slick quill pen

The 13_{th} amendment
abolished slavery they say
except for all those
in jail today

And somebody wrote
it wouldn't be cruel
to withhold from those people
their acres and their mule

It's written you know
they're shiftless and lazy
to give them their due
would be downright crazy

Because they don't read
and they sure don't write
so they'll fork it over
without a fight

Yeah, the pen can be lethal
a weapon treacherous.
Even more so
when the writer is lecherous

For those who don't write
or read what is written
Ignorance will leave you
in the cold frost-bitten

Best arm yourself
with literacy, my friend
and be quick on the draw
with your mighty pen

Be quick to draw
the mighty pen

January 1996

Aging

The years they come a creeping
a seeping and sweeping along
and Arthur come to right us
for eating and drinking wrong

Now my memory it's a skipping
cause my thoughts don't come as fast
as the names and dates and places
that keep slipping from my past

See my hair has turned to silver
And my teeth are filled with gold
plus my skin seems to wrinkle
as every year unfolds

Now my eyes started failing
can't see those tiny words
and my ears aren't hearing soundly
What's that? Don't think I heard

But the laughter hasn't left me
and there's joy still in my soul
cause at last I accept me
Aging—not getting old

January 2005 Written on my birthday…

Remember Me

Remember me not,
when I slipped and fell,
but for the funny little stories,
I used to tell.

When you remember me please,
recall those times, I used to tease,
and laugh and joke.
Remember I was just good folk.

Remember not to cry too long.
I loved myself,
I loved my song.

Remember when you speak of me,
how we were friends, and glad to be.
Remember not to grieve and moan,
for though I go, it's not alone.

Remember the quickness of my smile,
as we walk together this last mile.
You made my short stay worth while.

Remember I'll always love you,
and I *pray*, you'll always,
Remember me...

Voices of Civil Rights

In January of 1965, I had just turned 13 years old. Each of those years had been spent growing up in the first black public assistance housing projects in America. It was located, maybe 40 city-blocks from the White House, in Washington DC. By that time it had already deteriorated into a reject rather than a project. Abject poverty is what it was. I was considered among my peers as bright and articulate and culturally conscious. I was a firm believer in every word that came out of Malcolm X's mouth and would follow Martin Luther King Jr. into a fiery furnace. My heart and mind burned with a passion to change the world and right the injustices delivered by the hands of white supremacy and racism. Not only were we demanding civil rights but we were also proclaiming our Human Rights as citizens of the world. We had a cause.

And then came the heroin! All of a sudden, heroin was seen on every corner nodding its ugly head. As I look back it seemed as though the entire neighborhood was hooked over a span of 3 to 5 years. By 1970, the culture flame had flickered down to a spark. When Doctor King was murdered in 1968 and we decided to burn down all of our own neighborhoods, the one guy in the hood who remained steadfast and prosperous was the "Dope Man". There is a line in a poem that reads, "has the flame of our passion been blown out by drugs?" The answer is Yes. If it wasn't completely blown out, it certainly was diminished from a flame to a flicker.

When I hear or read anything concerning the civil rights movement, I seldom hear anyone dealing with this not only pertinent, but central issue. I think a commission should be appointed to find out who provided our neighborhoods with these movement-killing, illicit drugs and they should be prosecuted to the fullest extent of the law. Reflect on this, in the same neighborhood I'm referring to, you will find no less than 10 liquor stores within a four-square-block radius. That's criminal any way you look at it. Just imagine where we could be as a people, if our zealous hearts and fruitful minds had not been doused with all those poisonous elixirs.

When you talk about the "Voices of Civil Rights", just remember that hundreds of thousands of those Voices in every major city throughout this country were quieted and their vocal chords muted by dousing the owners with heroin, cocaine and alcohol. I wish someone would investigate that. Considering that we now have a black president in the seat of power I would think this is something we should explore. At least let's have a dialogue so we can hear some of those voices.

June 2004, written in response to a query from AARP's "Voices of Civil Rights" program.

When I Think of Malcolm

When I think of Malcolm, I think of confrontation. I think of the freedom associated with pure, unadulterated confrontation. I think of calling a spade a spade. I am absolutely certain that chickens really do "come home to roost" and I pity the person who would argue against the pragmatic wisdom contained in that simple phrase. I think of liberation and freedom in confrontation. If there is a festering sore, it needs to be confronted. There needs to be some active aggression against the lesion itself and the elements that caused the abrasion in the first place. Malcolm was an open act of aggression, attacking the wound that is racism and white supremacy.

When I think of Malcolm, I think of an altercation with evil that would rather die than remain under the auspices of tyranny and misguided righteous indignation. I think of a dispute with evil itself. An evil that propped itself up over a people and declared, "I am your superior." I think of a martyr who laid his body down across the bog of slavery's vestiges that I might cross over the river to the land that was promised.

When I think of Malcolm, my chest swells with pride and I understand the phrase "by any means necessary." Freedom, by any means necessary. If I'm not mistaken, that was the same hue and cry of George Washington, Thomas Payne, Ben Franklin, John Hancock and all the rest of those who signed that declaration announcing their freedom and independence. It stands to reason, right up hard against it, that if it was good for them, it should be good for me. When I think of Malcolm I think of just that, that I am here to confront you on that fundamental human right. Explain how it was all right for them to obtain liberty "by any means necessary," but somehow it's not quite right for me? And please don't give me any of that "that was then, this is now" excrement, because freedom is freedom, I don't care when you cut it.

When I think of Malcolm, I feel as tall and most times taller than those infamous (not so gentle) men who confiscated this land. I feel taller because I know for certain I earned my keep. When I think of Malcolm, I even question the use of the word 'gentle' in conjunction with the word 'men' when referring to America's founding fathers. I don't think there was anything gentle about them. When I think of what was done to the indigenous people of this land and my folk being tarred, feathered, lynched and castrated, somehow the word gentle doesn't come to mind. When I re-member and re-mind myself of those days that I worked from *cain't see to can't see, sun up to sun down*, with no pay and very little to eat, somehow gentle doesn't quite cut the quick. It's just not the correct adjective. If gentle means to be kind, considerate, comforting, soft, calm, mild and tender, then I think those guys came closer to being Anti-Christ's than gentlemen.

When I think of Malcolm, I think of many thousands of warrior souls who spent their lives in the fight for freedom like Patrice Lumumba, Denmark Vesey, Nat Turner, Amiri Baraka, Paul Robison, Frantz Fanon, Mukhtar, Senghor, Muhammad Ali, Fannie Lou Hamer, Nelson Mandela, Noble Drew Ali, Marcus Mosiah Garvey, Elijah Muhammad, Imhotep, Shaka Zulu, Jesus, Joshua, Harriet Tubman, Che Guevara, Sojourner Truth, Frederick Douglas, Ida B. Wells, Booker T. Washington, the Tuskegee Airmen, George Washington Carver, Toussaint L'Overture, David Walker, Sampson, Shadrack, Meshack, Abednego, Henry Highland Garnet, Cinque¢, George Jackson, Huey P. Newton, Jonathan Jackson, Bobby Hutton, Geronimo, Moses, Fred Hampton, Emmett Till, the Scottsboro Boys, Cochise, Sitting Bull, Jamil Al-Amin (H. Rap Brown), Jeronimo Pratt, Sheik Anta Diop, John Henrik Clarke, Henry "Box" Brown, who mailed himself to freedom, and I think of Kunta Kinte, who just simply refused to be Toby even after his foot was cut off.

When I think of Malcolm, I think of articulate strength, in spite of every conceivable obstacle. I think of the indefatigable strength of green grass growing, struggling up through inner-city project concrete, unstoppable, durable, hardy, strong, resilient, and defiant. I think of what he did for me and how I soared on the wings of his audacity. When I think of Malcolm, I smile…do you?

MALCOLM on Reparations

"If you are the son of a man who had a wealthy estate and you inherit your father's estate, you have to pay off the debts that your father incurred before he died. The only reason that the present generation of white Americans are in a position of economic strength...is because their fathers worked our fathers for over 400 years with no pay... We were sold from plantation to plantation like you sell a horse, or a cow, or a chicken, or a bushel of wheat...All that money...is what gives the present generation of American whites the ability to walk around the earth with their chest out...like they have some kind of economic ingenuity.

Your father isn't here to pay. My father isn't here to collect. But I'm here to collect and you're here to pay".

El-Hajj Malik El-Shabazz (Malcolm X); November 23, 1964, Paris,

Slave Narratives
Conveyed to a Prodigal Son

Recollections from the Book of Ty

Colonel John Wesley (JW) Alford Age 78
Buffalo Soldier, Cheyenne Wyoming

I was born in a barn on a sugar plantation in Franklin Harvest, Louisiana in 1860. I caint 'member before, but from the time I's five I worked the cane fields from what they call 'caint see to caint see' and that is, 'fore dawn in the mornin', till after dusk at night. I worked a-long-side my Mama till I was about ten then I sprang up tall. Seems all I can 'members 'bout them times was workin'. Sun-up till sun-down, seven days a week, just workin'.

I 'members Machete-Mack, they called him that cause he was the fastest man in Louisiana with that cane-knife o-his. He was 'bout seven foot-tall, weighed over three hundred pounds and, honest to God, they was no extra fat no-where's on his body. When he step in your path seem like the sun would go down, he was so big. They say big Machete-Mack could shuck a-acre-a-day by his self, when he was in a whistling mood. Powerful man, he was, who whistled while he worked.

I run away from them cane-fields when I was twelve years old. I lit out on a hot summer night, when the moon was high and full. I followed the North Star in a westerly direction. The notion come to me, that I rather git snake bit by a cotton-mouth, or mangled by a bayou-gator, then keep workin' for a monster what didn't even reckon I was human. It come to me at twelve that I rather die like a mangy dog, than be a slave. I knowed in my soul at twelve that weren't no man never born to be a slave to another man and I sooner die in the quick-sand swamp then let the devil steal my soul. So I lit out. I lit out, wit out so much as even tellin' my Mama. Freedom will pull you to it once you git a hankerin' for it.

I lived like John the Baptist off fruits, nuts, berries and grains for more than three years as I trekked my way through Oklahoma, Kansas, Colorado, Nebraska and Wyoming. I learned to live off the land and by the time I's fifteen I could catch a bass with grass nettle; I could trap a buffalo-bison with tree branches; and I had stared down a mean mountain lion. I could shinny up a tree and make shoes out of deer-hide. I shared honey and a cave with a family of black bears and tamed a golden Palomino named-o Sunshine.

I'm tellin' you this here story cause you need to know that I had a bunch-o-help from the Lawd, and a whole lot of help from peoples who knowed 'bout freedom. I gets help in my runnin' from the Creek's and the Apalache's whilst I's still in Louisiana. I gets help from the Choctaw and Arapaho in Oklahoma; and ten Delaware formed a human chain to pull me outta a twenty foot ravine I fell in tryin' to get outta the way of a surly swarm of Kansas yellow jack bees. I's cornered near a slope with no way to escape but offen' a hundred foot cliff near Boulder Colorado when a Shoshoni put a arrow in the hind-parts of a three hundred pound warthog, what had a mind to make me his meal. I got help from the Comanche, the Dakota and the Iowa tribes whilst I's in Nebraska and the Cheyenne/Algonquin's adopted me as their own. In later years I even traveled east a thousand miles or more and was put up for more than a year by a renegade band of North Carolina Cherokee's.

I feels the need here to 'splain to you how I come to be a Colonel in the United States Army and ain't never so much as served a day in one of them uniforms.

I members it was a fine spring day in 1898 and I's maybe twenty to thirty miles north of Laramie. I come upon a bluff that looked down over a ravine, what had a drop of maybe fifty feet or more. And they was five U.S. soldiers trapped 'twixt the ravine drop, the Laramie River and two hundred painted Cheyenne. I had tamed a big black stallion name-o-Midnight and he was a snortin' and a stompin' like he knowed death was in the air. The horse knowed the truth of it too, 'cause them Cheyenne was hell-bent for leather and intendin' on pealin' the scalp back on all five of them blue-coats. I aint gotta tell you how many of they tribe had been mistook and abused by them blue-eyed savages. We all knowed they had been released from hell to finish what Satan done started, and they aint had no friends in the entire territory. But I 'membered my Mama tellin' me way back in them cane-fields, she say "You don't swap evil for evil cause you caint win in the trade." And besides, she say almost every day, "Them white mens aint our teachers."

So somethin' come over me; I aint rightly sure what, but it was a powerful hankerin'. So me and Midnight rid down to the mouth of the ravine, betwixt the Cheyenne and the Yellow-Hairs and just stood betwixt 'em. Me and that horse just stood there lookin' at RainHawk and two hundred painted-for-war, intent to kill red-mens. I just stayed there, sittin' in my saddle and stared at 'em, must-o-been most of the mornin', and aint not word pass betwixt none of us. RainHawk, after a time, nodded at me and turnt his war-party. I 'members lookin' all five of them Calvary to the eye and aint never said a word. They nodded they 'preciation and mozied on outta of that pass.

Now thinkin' back to it, it was pert near a year or betta a'fore this here brigade of about thirty soldiers rid up to my cabin and called for me to come out. When I did, a Brigadier General named-o-Winston; he presented to me, all formal-like, these here golden-polished Colonel Wings and a Blue Coat wit a Colonel's ensign on it. He give me a salute and I give him a nod. He say, "Colonel John Wesley Alfred, it is my honor to appoint you as a officer and a gentlemen into the 9th Calvary, Buffalo Soldier Brigade of the United States Army. He give another salute, I looked him hard to the eye and give him another nod. He mounted his steed and rid away. Now, I heerd stories over the years 'bout how Buffalo Soldiers was Injun fighters, and it would make me sad, cause I aint never fought a one. I loved 'em all my life.

And now thinkin' back on it; I 'member I placed them gold wings on the mantel of my fireplace and I'd look at 'em from time to time. And I also 'members what I did wit that blue coat. Soon as the first chill come up over the rise I took it into the barn and laid it cross Midnights neck, and you know, that Blue coat served that horse a whole lot better than it ever served me, or my peoples.

Ignatious Holloway age 100 – Briar County, North Carolina

My name is Ignatious Holloway but pert near all my life, folks call me Ignant. Not cause I is ignant, they just like makin fun o my name, plus that's all Massa Trent ever called me was Ignant, and black folk always tryin to do what the white folks do.

I cain't rightly recollect when I started answerin' to Ignant, guess I always did. I's born a slave on a chicken farm in Briar County North Carolina. I 'spect I's seen the worst there is to see in this life. I reckon I's hatched on the worst spread a slave could ever draw if'n he had his druthers. I says that cause Massa Trent Livingston was mayhap the evil'st man ever what drawed a breaf. 'Specially if'n he was in his licka. The more he drank, the meaner he got. I think the better word for Massa Trent was cruel. He aint like nothin' nor nobody and whip ever thing what come in his path, 'cludin' his women's and his dogs. He whupped a slave a day and sometimes two iffen' he gotta mind. When I talk wit church folk they gasp for breaf and cross they self at the mere mention o the goin's on over to the Livingston Farm.

See Massa Trent wasn't the richest white man in the county, to set the facts, he was scroungin' right 'round close to the poorest. BessyMae say he was the 'no-count white-trash' o his kind, that every body knowed it, and that he was as close to the 'Devil's Ploughshear' as any human had ever come.

I knowed it first hand. He used to work me like a dog. I mean actual, like a dog. He used to fetch me from my shanty afore day in the mornin' wit his whip and his flask. His breath be smellin' like corn mashin's for light in the sky, thats the truth. We take to the woods down by the creek and iffen he spot a possum or coon or duck, he have me to git down to my hands and knees so he could use my back to level his aim wit that squirrel rifle o hissen. Iffen he hit his target I's usually pleased cause all I had to do was fetch it to him. That is, I's pleased iffen it won't shot over the river. I ain't never been much o' one for swimmin' but if the game was shot over the water, then I was the one what had to swim in to fetch it. That man so mean that iffen he miss what he was aim 'in at, then I gets the blame for it. My back lashed way up cause o all the times the rabbit won the game. Truth is I aint been able to walk straight up for more than 60 year or better, thats the reason you see me all bent over this way.

But I does remembers clear, the very last day of Massa Trent's drinkin' or huntin'. He come down to the quarters 'round day break. He holla for me but I don't come out. He come in drunk, shoutin' for me to get my lazy black ass up, "we's headed for the hills to catch some deer meat," he say. Well I's powerful sick wit the fever so bad he must o seen it in my eyes. I had swum in the river two days afore and I think it had just catched up to me. He holla's "you best get your black ass better afore tomorra cause ain't gonna be no sick 'scuses." He go on off to the woods mumblin' and almos staggerin' drunk, for daybreak I d'clare.

That night, round mid-night or so, his Missus come down to the quarters askin' is I see'd him. I told her what time he left, and she look at me hard to see the truth in me. I'm 'spectin' she seed it cause she just walk back to the big house. Next mornin' she back sayin' somethin' aint right an we gotta go look for him. Well, we put together a small search party and we look most all that day and ain't find him nowheres. Well then the rumor starts that he done run off to Virginy or somewhere wit some white trash, so we stopped lookin'. It was zactly two days later we see the buzzards circlin' off to the north of where we usual hunt and we knowed it was trouble.

This time we brung the dogs when we searched to put a scent-trail on him. And we fount Massa Trent Livingston almost torn ‘pletely apart from the looks of him. Either a bear or a mountain lion or sompin’ mean done took holt of him, an tore him limb from limb, literal. It mayhap the worse thing I seen in all my livin, the way he was ripped open an all. Bugs was eatin’ all in his eyes and vermin had started feastin’ on his innards. We had to shoe ’em off. If it waren’t for his clothes we woulda neva knowed it was him. All I could think was, he got good as he gave. As I recollect, we gathered up much of ‘em as we could, to bring him back for a proper Christian burial and all. And I swear by all that I knowed is sacred, that as we was walkin’ back through the pass wit Massa Trent in tow, I seent a smile on the Missus Trent’s face…

Bathsheba Hempstead, Over 90 – Sumter, South Carolina

I's christened Bathsheba Hempstead and even though I's a good ways pass 90, my memry serve me like sweet serve a tater with 'lasses on it. I was almost sold two times on account o my high spiritness. Niggra folk say I had too much gumption for to be a slave. I spect I 'gree wit em, cause I ain't never liked nothin' bout slavery. Nothin'! Still in all, wit all my gumption, that's all I ever was, a slave. I was born and raised on a breedin' plantation near Sumter South Carolina. My mammy had 20 childrens in 22 years. I was the tenth of em. Folk use to brag on me beatin' her record cause I spit out 23 in the same mount of time.

Now I kilt the daddy of my first born's b'fore they got here. But let me splain to you why. Massa Collins, who we b'long to, sent a big black John-Buck name-o-Sam in at me when I had just seent my fifteenth birthday. He say, the Massa done 'clared I his woman, this here's a niggra breedin farm and he gone have his way wit me.' Well, I fight and tare at his flesh wit my fingers and my feets till I's plum tuckered. I screams and holla's and cries till the water in my head dried up. That big niggra wrestled and tussled wit me nigh on to an hour b'fore I collapse from tuckeration, and he complish his evilment.

Now you needs to know that I begged and pleaded wit him not to touch me, and I had asked him p'litely as any young Negress gal can, not to touch me. But he did. He tore my 'ginity open, to where I was bleedin', and it pained me to tarnation. He pound up and down on me till I faint dead away. I spect he must of thought my faintin' was consentment cause when I come to, this here fool is sleep and snorin' like a bull after cow servicein'.

My mammy always said I was born wit a mean streak that the devil hisself was affeared of. Well, I don't know bout that, but I do knowed I marched out o that cabin, went straight to the wood shed and grabbed the first thing I seed, which was a pickaxe. I stomped right back in there where the fool was still snorin. I mustered all the hurt, pain and evil that was in me; and I planted that pickaxe, pick side, right plum in the middle o his chest. I left it right there where I planted it; went down to the troff and tried to wash out the gissm he shot up in me; walked up to the Massa's house, looked him straight to his eye and tolt him what I just done.

Now I seent Massa Collins whup clear pass a hundred slaves whilst I's on his plantation and I knowed a few of 'em died as the result of it. But it ain't never come no wheres near my thinkin' that he might whup me for my temper comeuppance. I sposen' he aint never thought of it neither, cause he ain't never laid a finger nor a bull's hide to me for what I done to that there John-Buck. Massa just look at me and say, "Sheeba, you done cost me a heep and you best b'leeve you gone make me a heep." That's all he say.

Next mornin' I's called out early by the Massa's Missis who always was kind to me and treated me half human. She ask me which one o the field-hands I took a shine to. I tolt her, "I likes Big Henry Hempstead fine." That next Saddy evenin' me and Henry jump the broom at dusk. And just pass 9 months to the week, I livered twin girls. And every year for the next 21 straight years I brought a child in this world. 21 of em was boys, the first 2 was girls. Recollectin' back to it, I spose Massa Collins was right cause them 23 childrens was a heap o' pay for that one big John-Buck. And y'all wanna know sump'n; each and every one o my childrens look just like big Henry Hempstead, ceptin' them first 2 twins.

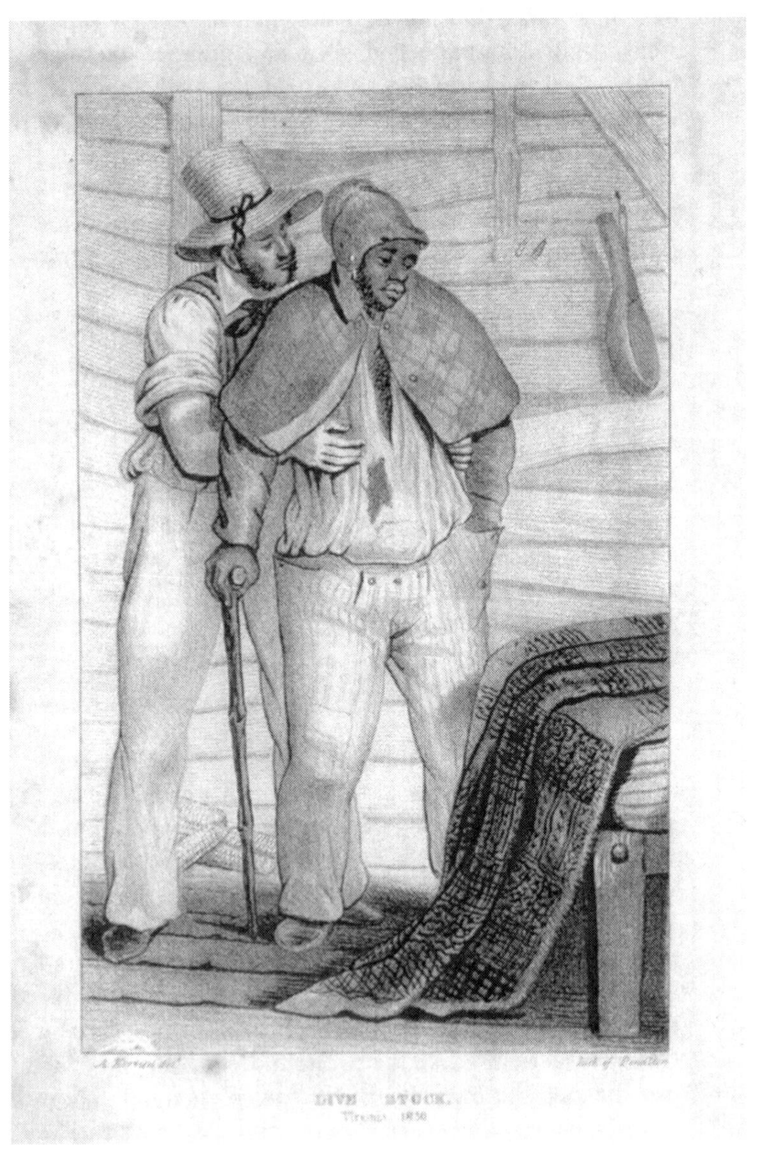

LIVE STOCK.

Ebenezer Carter, age 93
Rain, Tennessee

I overheer'd conversment twixt some a them abo-lish-nist. You know, thems the good white folk what was wantin' to 'bolish slavery all along. One says to the other, "I 'clare I don't know how the Niggra peoples can stay so full o merriment and jollification. 'Spite o they conditions, theys always a laughin' and a jokin' when they aint workin', and sometimes even when they is."

The other says to the one, "I 'spect its cause you can enslave they bodies, but you caint enslave they souls."

Now over the years I give that talk some con'sidiation in spells. And I reckon my mind and my body been torn ever-which-away. I been whupped for learning to read and my offspring took from me. I was solt two times down river. I been hungry from the miss-meal cramps. I done had the misery, been angry, I been sad and even mad as hell on a few o'ccasions. But ya know, in more then ninety years top side o this here earth, I reckon them white mens is just a little too mean to understand, but I ain't never had no problem findin' some joy in my soul…Ha, ha, ha, ha…

Paco Suarez Hope-Tale of the Texas Troubles Age 98 Amarillo, Texas

I was born a slave on a cattle spread near Austin Texas that was one hundred thousand acres wide and had more than ten thousand head a Long-Horn on it. My first memory is of a stampede where my mama and eight of my kinfolk was kilt in the commotion.

My mama was a slave from Tupelo Mississippi and my daddy was a Mexican soldier what had deserted Santa Anna's army to be wit my mama 'cause the love-bug had bit him so bad; least wise that's the story they give me. They say my daddy was kilt in a knife-fight over a dispute at a card game and my mama tossed sulfur-acid in the eyes of the fellow what done it, and blinded him for true.

Now the clearest memory I has is on the day I's branded. The Hopes branded all they stock; they hosses; they steers; they sheeps and they slaves. I growed up on the Hope cattle ranch and I 'members my uncle Charlie say one day, when I's twelve years old, "I bleeve that boy done shot up almost a foot in one summer," and the day after he said it I was took to the brandin' barn and cuffed in the witches-stock, where the Double-H was 'plied to my right shoulder. I members I screamed till my head went black and I waked up when they poured a tin of salt-brine on it. Aint nobody look me to the eye for a long while after, as I recalls it. They is a lot a shame in slavery.

I was tolt that in 1825 the Hope's was 'lowed eight thousand acres-o-land cause the government give 'em eighty acres for evy one bonded slave they bought to Texas wit 'em, and by the time I's born twenty years later, they's spread done growed to over one hundred thousand acres. They's high and mighty, the Hope's was. I was tolt that the year I's born, in eighteen and forty; is the year Texas join the Union, and that they was more than thirty thousand bonded slaves-a-workin' by that time. It was further tolt to me that just five years later, they was almost double that, and that by the time I is fifteen years old in 1860, they was more than one hundred and eighty thousand slaves workin Texas land.

Now I'm tellin' you all these here figures, cause I wants you to know, that from the very day they branded me wit that there double H hot iron, I commenced to workin' 'gainst slaveholders and all they devilish ways. And I set my life to the 'bolishment of it. They called it they Peculiar Institution and I called it my Particular Hell.

At fifteen years old I come to the period in my livin', where's I made up my mind I could no longer, nor never again be a bondsmen to another man. I rather die then be a slave; and come to the notion that I was gone get free by any means whatsoever. It make me chuckle-a-mite sometimes when I think of it, cause I was tolt that it was actual said down in the Austin Legister House, by one of they lawmakers that, and this here's a quote; he say "Our slaves are the happiest of human beings-on who the sun shines." I guess he was 'ferrin to Texas slaves over maybe say, Carolina one's. I don't know who that man was talkin' 'bout. I knowed he wasn't 'ferrin to me!

To prove he weren't 'ferrin' to me I lit out from the double H on the first day of April in 1860. Me, Big Jesse, Blacksmith Sam, Matthew Austin and Lazy Watson. I members they called him that cause he worked so hard, harder then any two mules. Lazy, weren't even lazy at all. Its funny how peoples get they names.

Anyway, we had done laid the plot for escape six months back, and took to runnin' at the first spring rain. We headed north through Temple, Killeen, Waco and Fort Worth before we settled on Dallas. We met a few good a'bolitionist on the way who helped us with viddles and transport papers and the like. That's when I learned that not all of 'em was evil. I think it may have been the hottest summer I recollect ever livin' through. It was so hot that Lazy cooked a dozen eggs on a flat-rock one afternoon. Ha, ha, ha…

One day, it was July 7 to be exact, they was a big ruckus to beat all get out, and a lynch-mob rounded-up two slaves and three white mens and brung 'em to the town square. The vigilantes hung the two slaves right whilst the sun was high, and then they took the three white a'blistionist and tied 'em face-down, with they belly's layin' 'cross a empty hoss troff. They cut open them mens shirts and commence to stripin' 'em wit one hundred lashes each wit a cat-o-nine-tails. They beat them mens so long that they had to take turns a doin it. When they's finished, they leaves 'em layin', backs-a-bleedin', cross that hoss troff and tolt everybody within hearin' that if they help them, then they was gone suffer the same out-come. Next mornin' we seed that during the night some spawns-o-Satan had done thowed leeches on they backs and suck the blood right up out 'em. Ump!

And that is the day the Texas Troubles started in earnest. I cain't rightly x'plain the heaviness that come over my heart as I looked at them mens, the two that was hangin' and the three slumped over the troff. At the same time that heaviness come, a meaness come wit it. A meaness that was so set on getting' even wit that mob, that for-a-time, I couldn't even see straight. We all had been layin' our minds to how we was gone put a end to slavery, but the savageness of them vigilantes was what put the spark to it.

Big Jesse and me had stole two wagon loads of kerosene and we got five crates of 'prairie-matches' from Fort Worth. We had also got ten kegs-o-black powder from the stock-pile at the Fort. Peoples don't know that the slaves was always the ones who handled all the powder and the shells anyway, cause white men's was a-feared of it. Specially them new-fangled "prairie-matches" they was no tellin' when them things would just spark-up on they own.

On July 8th 1860 on a hot star-filled night, I lead twenty-five mens on a barn-fire that the state of Texas never will forget. I 'members how I rubbed that double H brand on my shoulder and recalled the heat that surged thru my body at high noon three years b'fore, and got to thinkin', 'I'm fittin to brand me some folk wit some hot irons tonight.'

Big Jessie and Lazy led ten mens-a-pourin kerosene, layin' powder and plantin' matches at the south end of the city limits. Blacksmith Sam and Matt Austin led the rest from the north end. They covered almost every back porch and barn; all the livery's and general stores; all the houses and hotels; every place they could spread the potion, they spread it. Then we's all, everyone of us, put white sheets on like Klan, got on horse back, lit torches and commenced to burnin'. The fire spread so fast in some places due to the con-coction that some folks weren't even able to escape they quarters. Now I hope the Lawd forgive me for this, but I ain't never lost a night of sleep as the result of it.

We kept ridin' north and burnin'. We burnt up Dallas, Denton, Pilot's Point and Union City b'fore the sun come up. I members big Lazy sayin', just afore we got started, in that slow way he used to talk; "its gon be a hot time in the old town tonight." I guess you could say, we raised hell that night. I 'members readin' some twenty-or-so years later that white folk wouldn't never admit that some slaves had started the Texas Troubles. They said that the fires was started cause-o-them new-fangled matches had, what they called 'spontaneous combusted' ha, ha, ha. Them white folks aint want to give black folks credit for nothin'. I means nothin'. They aint think we was smart enough to out-smart them in nothin'. They must think that some folks is stupid iffen' they want you to believe that four different Texas cities in one night caught fire do to some fickle prairie matches…ha, ha, ha.

Now I know the history books says one thing but, they is a lotta lies in them books, and I'm here to tell you the truth of it. It still give me some pleasure, even at this ripe old age of 98 years, cause I actual lived through it; as a matter of fact, it give me a whole lot of pleasure cause aint nothin' nobody can do 'bout it now. I want every man within hearin', colored or white, that ever thought about brandin' another man with a hot iron; I want y'all to know that it was me; IT WAS ME, a fifteen year-old son of a slave and a Mexican Bandito, what burnt down Dallas, and was THE CAUSE of all your Texas Troubles.

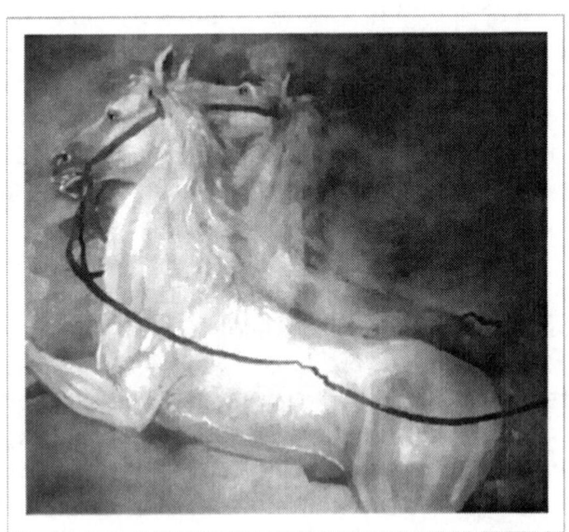

Cyrus James age 90
Lookout Mountain, Georgia

I d'clare I aint never knowed what make them white folks mean as they is; so full a hate and misery and all. I seen wit my own eyes Massa Greely, over to the Augusta Peach Plantation, shoot a slave to the gut what had eat a peach offen a tree. That slave had worked from afore day to the dusk and hadn't eat nothin' all that day. I swear for Gawd in heaven, I cain't unerstan how a man could kill another man over a peach. Hell, they was peaches plenty on the orchard, so many you could see the trees 'clare pass the 'rizon all the way to the Georgia line...Oomph, oomph, oomph…

Amos Sweeney Aged 77 Philadelphia PA

In the year of our Lord in 1870 I found myself in the employ of, and providin' janitorial and wait services to, one Thomas Alva Edison; but more particular to the issue and relevant to the fact, I was blessed to be assigned to the right, reverent, gentleman, Mr. Louis H. Latimer his self.

And I must state before all within hearin' that, as a free man born the son of a slave, I could not of been mo proud of the position that the Lawd had 'ranged, for I found myself workin' for one of the most brilliant human bein's that God had ever created, and the mere fact that he was Black caused my chest to swell like a rooster's.

You see, Mr. Latimer was a scientist what would come up wit notions 'bout things. He had all kinds of inventions runnin' round in his head. He seemed a might surly and even strange sometimes, but it was knowed by us all that he was the smartest man in the entire world. That man could figure out ever thing, and I means that genuine, ever thing. He just knowed how stuff worked. I mean stuff most folk don't know. Like how 'tricity worked. He knowed it. How the sun and the moon timed theyself. He knowed it. How gravity 'plied itself to things. He just knowed it. All the rich and important white mens come to him for stuff. They all did, and you got me as a witness to it.

That Mr. Alexander Graham Bell would always come to him needin' an answer for things, and he just hand it right to him, wit out even so much as blinkin' his eyelids. Just smart, he was. And let me tell y'all this; Mr. Edison could not have done nothin' if it weren't for Louis, cause his mind was just pure reckonin'. I mean it was just like the Lawd was sittin' terectly on his forehead waitin' wit answers. Mercy, Mercy.

I traveled all over wit Mr. Latimer, I did, but he wouldn't let us call him that. He aint like that, he say his name was Louis and he weren't no betta than any of us Hands, what worked the factories and the labs. Now he was a very serious man when it come to 'bolishin' slavery. He had left school early in his life and helped his family by sellin' the anti-slavery newspaper journal called, the Liberator. He was serious 'bout freedom for black folk, he was.

But like I said, we traveled all over. And some of the younguns' in ear-shot of me, don't even know that it was me, what put up the first street-lights in New York, in Philadelphia where we's sittin' here now, and up yonder in Canada and over the water to that there London, England too. Yep, under the super-visory issue of Mr. Louis Howard Latimer.

I 'members he would be up late in the night workin' on things. Things folks is takin' for granted today. It was him what help Mr. Alexander Bell wit that telephone machine we's usin' everywhere now. I 'members the night he handed him the drawin' for it, and Mr. Bell thanked him fifty times, iffen' he thanked him once. I seed and heered that myself!

I members one spring night in 1881, I recollect the weather was hot for spring. Louis and a few of us lab-hands, the most of which was colored mens like me; we's all excited cause he done come up wit the electric light. Folks later talkin' 'bout he co-invented it with Mr. Edison, it weren't no co-nothin'. That man had figured that whole thing out and then invite the rest of us in when he done finished the figurin'. It was a happy night too, 'cause he had done worked on it since pre-historic, seemed like. We's all got tipsy that evenin' drinkin' corn-mashin's wit viddles, and listenin' to the phonograph, which he helped think up too.

Now like I said, that man was pure genius walkin', as I'm thinkin' back to it. I members we was on a train headed west from Pennsylvania one evenin' and Louis looked at me powerful long and he say, "Amos, I don't think its right that we gotta hold ourselves and wait for the next stop ever time we gotta pee. Somebody aught to do somethin' 'bout that." Then he started lookin' up in the air, like he done regular, when he was ponderin' on somethin'. And I knowed it was somethin' comin'. Soon as we got to Chicago he rush to the lab and drawed up the first blue-print-drawin' for the water-closet used on every train a runnin' today.

I 'members, ha, ha. I members quite a few years later, whilst I was actual using the water-closet, in a COLORED-ONLY car on the Baltimore and Ohio rail. I got to thinkin' 'bout the white folks up front in the FOR-WHITES-ONLY cars. And I's wonderin' would they had used them water-closets, if they knowed it was a black man what invented 'em? Ha, ha, ha…

Ethel Ann Hardison age 88
Lithonia, Louisiana

At age five or so I's sent up to the big house to work. My first memories is as a bed warmer in the fall and winter. I slept to the foot of the bed so the Massa and the Missus could put they cold feets on me. And in the spring and summer I slept on the floor and toted the fan everywhere the Missus went, so to keep her cool and the bugs offen her. I 'spect I's about eight or so when it was explained to me that I was a Mulatto Negress and that I was the child of a white man. It wasn't clear to me back then but it is clear to me nowadays, that I was the Massa's daughter. It don't make much never mind no way cause it never was owned up to by nobody, never. Nobody had the nerve to say that General Jebediah Buford A. Spragan would stoop to relations with a slave, even if it was knowed for miles around that my Mammy was the prettiest slave gal in the entire Parish and I look dead on just like the both of 'em.

Most of the field hands had the mistaken notion that I had it good cause I worked to the big house and they worked the fields. I would have gladly traded field work for them slop buckets any day. See I had to empty the slop jar every day, at least 3 times a day, for the Massa, the Missus and they three younguns, seven days a week. That is at least 15 times a day of truggin' down to the lime pit with stankin' pee and crap from the Massa, the Missus, Jeb Junior, Missy Ann and the young Massa Caleb. And if they was any guest stayin' over, well then I'd be totin' their's too.

The Massa's brother, Jacob come home from the war and took his way wit me when I's round fourteen or so. I know they heerd me screamin' in the beginning parts of it. I screamed till he knocked me out. When I come too, I's bleedin' all over Louisiana. I just clean myself up and ain't no body never spoke a word about it. He go on back off to the war some where and was kilt, I hear tell. I knowed I ain't never seent him again.

I cleaned the bed linen, washed the walls, cleaned the oven and cleaned the grill-pit. I cleaned the soot from the fireplace. I washed the windows, washed the dishes, washed the pots and washed the pans. I scraped the wax from the candle-holders, I swat the carpets, scrubbed and mopped the floors, cleaned the knobs on the doors, mend the curtains, dust the furniture and fed the dogs. I slopped the hogs and fed the chickens. I milked the cows and cleaned the troughs. I washed the clothes, darned the socks, sewed the sweaters and the coats. When I did the figurin' I 'spect I worked 18 to 20 hours a day. I worked till the gumption in my hands froze up and pained me to tears.

Nowadays I'm just prayin' that when I get on up to glory I ain't got no more cleanin' to do. I declare I done cleaned all I care to, in this here life time and I woulda traded the field for that big house and them slop jars any day.

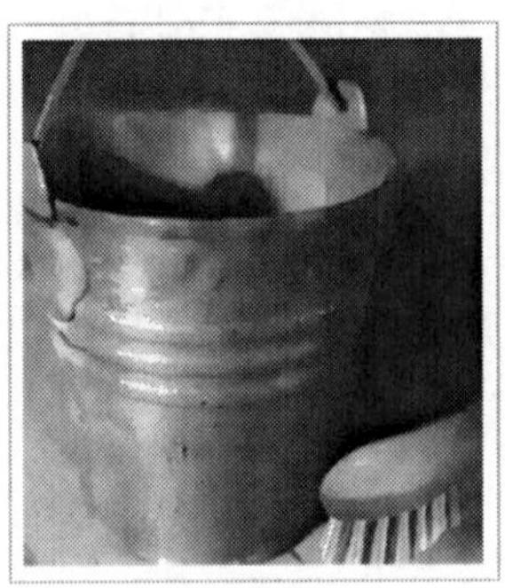

Thaddeus Whitmore age 99
Deep Hollow, Maryland

"You might find this hard to swallow but I believed that I was growed from a Giggaboo tree clear up till I was past 10 years old.

You see the Massa, the Missus and all they younguns that we played wit as children's, always told us that we was growed from Giggaboo trees. They told us that the good Niggra's what worked the fields, obeyed they Master, knew they God given place and prayed to the Lawd for they deliverance; they was growed from the Giggaboo tree.

But the bad Niggra's what would run off trying to escape, and the real evil Niggra's what would talk back to they owners and rebel against they natural superior's, like that there Nat Turner, why they was hatched from buzzard eggs.

And I believed both of them tales clear up to the time I was ten years old. I members it well cause that was the day I helped LulaMay 'liver her first born son, Jacob. She was fourteen and I was ten. That's the first time I figured out that some-o-them white folks was liars…"

Hannibal Haskins, age 101
Bristol, Florida

You know what pains me all the way to the marrow in my bones? Is the way the peoples of today talk about themselves; my peoples. It pains my heart terrible to come the notion that after all we worked, sweated and died for, folk would actual call themselves by the names we hated. Why do you 'spect them Slavers went to so much trouble to stop you from using your own African names and forced you to use the names they give us.

I seent with my own two eyes, folk get they feets and they fingers cut off for using they home country talk. I witnessed a man get his member whacked off in front of 75 slaves for tellin' a story 'bout how beautiful Africa was. I seen it!

Folk died by the thousands not to be called Nigger and here you is volunteerin'. Callin' your women folk the same as dogs. It's terrible. I heard 2 overseers at a PicNic Party (that's where all the Slavers would bring food and liquor in baskets to a festive gatherin' to buy, sell, trade and pick they slaves) most folk don't even know that's where the term 'picnic' come from. Anyway, I heard one say to the other, that this here slave gal wasn't worth no more than his female blood hound cause she was 16 and still hadn't had no litter. He say, "at least that bitch could hunt," in re'ferin' to the dog.

I 'members when it would be a fight to the death for calling a black woman a bitch. Now yawl got it in your songs. Lord Jesus-a-Mercy!

I 'spect my Mammy would flip over faced down in her grave if she knew what this world had come to…

The Lynching of Sam Hose
Author Unknown

On Sunday afternoon, April 23, 1899, more than 2,000 white Georgians, some of them arriving from Atlanta on a special excursion train, assembled near the town of Newman to witness the execution of Sam Hose, a black Georgian. Alfred Cranford, his white employer, had threatened him with a gun and Hose had thrown an ax in self-defense and the ax struck Cranford in the skull, killing him.

Within two days, the newspapers had dreamt up an altogether different scenario: Cranford had been eating dinner when Hose—"a monster in human form"—sneaked up on him, buried an ax in his skull, and after pillaging the house, dragged Mrs. Cranford into the room where her husband lay dying and raped her. Mob justice would mete out the punishment for this mythical crime: After stripping Hose of his clothes and chaining him to a tree, the self-appointed executioners stacked kerosene-soaked wood high around him. Before saturating Hose with oil and applying the torch, they cut off his ears, fingers, and genitals, and skinned his face. Some in the crowd plunged knives into the victim's flesh. Others watched, with unfeigned satisfaction, the contortions of Sam Hose's body as the flames rose, distorting his features, causing his eyes to bulge out of their sockets, and rupturing his veins. The only sounds that came from the victim's lips, even as his blood sizzled in the fire, were, "Oh, my God! Oh, Jesus."

Before Hose's body had even cooled, his heart and liver were removed and cut in to several pieces and his bones were crushed into small particles. The crowd fought over these souvenirs. Shortly after the lynching, one of the participants reportedly left for the state capital, hoping to deliver a slice of Sam Hose's heart to the governor of Georgia, who would call Sam Hose's deeds "the most diabolical in the annals of crime."

I inserted this story from an unknown author simply because this is only one in hundreds of thousands, maybe even millions, of stories that have not been told nor have they been dealt with. It showcases the heinous crimes committed against black people in this country. I bring it to your attention because people need to understand the depth of the pain we suffer and just how hurtful it is and has been. To be subjugated to these criminal acts and never apologized to for them has left indelible scars on the hearts and in the minds of a large percentage of this country. The pain and suffering does not go away simply because it is not acknowledged. As a matter of fact the denial exacerbates and makes the hurt appear to be worse than it would be if it were addressed.

African American descendents of former slaves need closure. The above incident is a microcosm of the macrocosmic stain left by the blood of my people. It is an open wound to the majority of us because the vestiges of these acts are like a miasmic cloud hovering over our heads every day. The residue of this evil can be seen all over the urban areas of the north, south, east and west and the only way for us to get up from under this cloud is to first acknowledge that it exists. We need to be able to forgive because it is impossible to forget. We need dialogue. We need closure.

After reading and seriously considering all the above, is it any wonder that it takes a great deal of strength to make a black woman smile.

A Black Woman's Smile

Do you know how strong you have to be
to make a black woman smile?
Do you have any idea what an accomplishment that is?
She has borne the weight of this country on her back
for 400 years.
She's been carrying the load of America in her belly
since its infancy.
She has suffered the agony of unassisted, husband-less
child-rearing since the 1600's.
Have you any idea how much strength it takes
to put a smile on her face?
You need the strength of Sampson, the nerve of Joshua
and the courage of David facing Goliath.
Cause she has cultivated in her womb
the marvel of the universe,
only to have her hopes and dreams aborted
and her aspirations show up dead on arrival.
She has given birth to kings and queens
and delivered on her majestic promise
only to have her children kidnapped and sold
to a criminal with no respect for her royalty.
If you can make a black woman smile,
you are a miracle worker.
Imagine breastfeeding your child in Virginia
and having him snatched from your arms, branded;
hijacked to Louisiana and publicly fondled
on a New Orleans auction block.
If the memory of that pain was locked-bound
in your DNA, would you be smiling?
If you breast-fed someone else's child
only to watch her grow old enough to call you Darky,
Pickaninny and Nappy-headed Jigaboo,
you wouldn't be smiling either.
If you <u>can</u> make a black woman smile
you have DONE something.

If you can make her smile
you are stronger than Atlas,
cause God knows she has been.
She's been raped and ravaged and scorned...
and nearly annihilated.
She's been pimped and pummeled and stoned...
and deliberately depreciated.
She has cooked and cleaned and sewn…
and never been compensated.
She's been forced to watch the offspring of her loins
mangled and maligned across centuries.
Her character has been continuously smeared,
assassinated over and over and over;
again and again and again.
You ever thought about how strong you have to be,
just to BE a black woman?
She's had to make brick without straw
after being…stripped of all her customs,
stripped of all her culture, stripped of all her traditions.
No other woman in the history of the civilized world
has gone through what she's gone through.
No other beings on the planet have endured
what she has endured.
She's been chastised, criticized,
demonized and terrorized.
She's had to stand when her man was bull-whipped
for trying to stand.
She's had to stand when her man was
castrated for trying to stand.
She's had to stand when her man was hung by his neck
for trying to stand.
She's had to carry her man, cause every time he tried to
carry himself, he was murdered for trying to do so.
Ask Betty Shabazz about Malcolm; ask Corretta Scott
King about Martin; ask Emmett Till's mother; ask
Medgar Evars wife.
If you can make a black woman smile
you have achieved something.

Since 1619 when we came in chains,
the entire world's been messing with her brain,
disrespecting her, calling her out of her name,
and she's tired…just plain Fanny Lou Hamer, tired…
Tired of being called B-words, and H-words and N-
words and other-words
and everything except the child of God that she is.
But…the one thing in this world that will make a black
woman smile…is her man...
A real man!
If you're doing what you're supposed to do…she will
smile…she will smile regularly and gladly.
So… man up my brother…
Man up and make your woman smile.
Treat her like the Queen that she is…
She deserves it…
And recognize this…
In all of God's Creation there is nothing more alluring,
more appealing, or attractive; nothing more beautiful.
There's nothing more charming, more charismatic, or
captivating, nothing more delightful, nothing more
elegant, or exquisite; nothing more fascinating, nothing
more gorgeous. There's nothing more inspiring, or
intoxicating. There's nothing more magnificent. There is
nothing more lovely than a Black Woman's Smile

EPILOGUE

At the core of all these thoughts is the spirit of triumph and achievement. Although I have expressed a great deal of irritation at some of the conditions we, African-Americans, undergo here in the United States, at the heart of it is a sense of victory. After all, and in spite of the many miserable atrocities, we have endured on these shores, we survive nevertheless.

Even with the deck heavily stacked against us, thrown into the game with little to no chips, and most times not even understanding the rules, we thrive. There is something noble and courageous to be said about that. So I am hopeful that the reader does not interpret this as anything but a testimonial to the indomitable strength of my people and pray that this serves as a reminder to everyone that there must be some dialog around these issues.

I also want to convey a sense of optimism to the descendants of slaves and an admonition to the descendants of slave holders, specifically those who have made an effort to keep us in bondage and servitude. The universal law of reciprocity and evolution says that the 'Cream Shall Rise' and we will, in due course, overcome as Dr. King declared. We cannot be destroyed and we will ultimately prevail. It would behoove America to make efforts to right the injustices that are present everywhere throughout this society. It is in America's best interest to repair the damages it has done. It makes sense for the United States to make amends because it is absolutely true what Malcolm said, "chickens do come home to roost."

In the schools of Africa, students are miss-educated about the African Diaspora and their brothers and sisters who were taken away to servitude in the West. And here in the West, students are not taught about their spiritual, cultural and blood connections to Africa. This kind of willful "miss-education" is racism/apartheid at its zenith. It is at the very heart of the problem, and it has to stop.

The black former slaves in America were stripped of all their customs, culture and traditions. A rootless tree can bear neither leaves nor fruit. The root must be planted deep in the soil and cultivated. Since our cultivation was cut off by design, the world's court should intervene and deal with those that stooped to such a crime. America should stand trial before the world for all the criminal atrocities it imposed upon black people the same as other heinous crimes against humanity are prosecuted. The trial would culminate with an open admission to the world, with complete apologies and punitive damage awards.

I'm not talking about handouts or charity. I'm talking about compensation, plain and simple. Fee Payment for services rendered with compounded interest. There is a debt that is owed and there is no statute of limitations. There is no statute of limitations on willful and premeditated murder. Black people should not 'hem and haw' nor quake in this demand for justice. Because it is just that, a demand for justice. The whole world is suffering because black people throughout the Diaspora were denied education, economic freedom, political recourse and social inclusion. When we look closely at the innumerable contributions people of African descent have made to American society in the fields of art, science, medicine, sports, literature, politics, etc. I wonder how much further along the country would be if Black's had not been deprived of the constitutional freedoms afforded to everyone else.

The world is suffering because, had these talents been nurtured instead of systemically and deliberately repressed, we probably would have cured cancer by now or learned to convert rainwater into automobile fuel. The world is suffering because the first inclination of Black people is to help, not harm and that humanitarian spirit has been manipulated and exploited. Instead of exploiting our proclivity, why not nurture it, develop it. If embraced, that benevolent spirit of caring and giving would permeate throughout this society and the citizens would naturally develop the same characteristics and the blessings would overflow for the benefit of mankind. But instead we have the opposite. Instead we have pursuers of war, willing to kill for the sake of crude oil. Instead of love, truth, peace and freedom we have a bunch of hurting people running around hurting people.

During 2004, in the Nation's Capital of the United States, twenty-three teenagers were murdered. The majority of those murders took place among the same descendants of those who were denied education, economic freedom, political recourse and social inclusion. The correlation is no accident. It is by design, yet these issues were not even subjects of political debate during that election year. There is a clear and obvious error in this and now is the time to correct it.

In 2010, while politicians speak of liberation, freedom and a brand new America, all the same old signs of Jim Crow and apartheid still exist along race and class lines. We are still very much a country fueled and sustained by slavery. In Loudon County Virginia, the state adjacent to the nation's capital, on December 16th 2009 every news channel carried reports of lynching nooses being hung in a black firefighter's car, as a prank, they say. Race haters burning crosses in the same state while the states of Texas and Oklahoma are seriously talking about seceding from the union because a black man, Barak Obama, is in the White House.

If one takes a critical look at the prison system, slavery takes a front row in the discussion. Eight out of ten prisoners are of African and Hispanic descent. If we represent 12 percent of the general population how on earth is it possible for us to represent 80 percent of the prison population? That's incredible, by any stretch of the imagination. If you examine closely and take a good hard look at why? you'll find one word. Labor! Labor! Labor! That is it in a nutshell.

If you peel back all the layers of ownership, you'll find that the same wealthy aristocrats who prospered from the free labor that came with owning slaves, are the same families and companies that thrive off the production of goods and services in the prisons where the labor is as close to free as you can get. Think about it, if you could get a man to make chairs that sell for two hundred dollars each on the open market and then pay that man next to nothing for making them, then you would find yourself sitting pretty too. The pun is intended.

Slavery is alive and well in America and no one wants to talk about it. As a matter of fact, anyone who makes an effort to talk about it is quickly maligned, criticized and ostracized. A prime example of this can be seen in the story of one of America's finest scholars, who was a prominent athlete, entertainer and human-rights leader, Paul Robeson.

In 1947 an organization called the American Heritage Foundation decided to tour the United States with the Declaration of Independence. Not a copy, but the original document. They planned to accomplish this grand tour on a magnificent locomotive called the "Freedom Train." This austere project was endorsed by then President Harry Truman and sponsored by the then Attorney General of the United States. However, there was a hitch in the giddy-up because the American Heritage Foundation would not assure and refused to guarantee that the exhibition would be desegregated. Well you can imagine that this really rubbed the African American community the wrong way, as well as those Caucasian people who had fought against segregation. How could you sincerely suggest a "freedom train" and at the same time, restrict the freedom of Black citizens (For Whites Only) to participate and ride on it.

Langston Hughes, upon learning of this miscarriage of justice, responded poetically to the national outcry of the African American community, who were understandably incensed by the contradiction. It stands to reason that the community would be upset as the exhibit was preaching freedom and equality while at the same time practicing apartheid and segregation. The title of the poem is "Freedom Train" which, to me, is one of Langston's most poignant pieces. After hearing and falling in love with the poem, Paul Robeson began performing it as a staple in his shows. During the late 1940s, he declared that he would never perform before a segregated whites-only audience again. For taking that stance against injustice, Paul's character was brought into question and he was ostracized for exercising his First Amendment Rights and refusing to accept anything less than equality. That was 63 years ago.

Today, in 2010, you have the same evil and villainous character assassination going on with another of our most prodigious contributions to this society, Amiri Baraka. The same powers that pooled their resources to assassinate the character of Paul Roberson then, are doing the exact same thing to Amiri today. Because he would dare to question America in his landmark and ingenious poem, (Somebody Blew Up America) they abolished the position of Poet Laureate in the state of New Jersey. Can you imagine? I don't know if there is any other state in the history of this country that has abolished its Poet Laureate position? Every person in this country and throughout the world should be outraged and incensed at the inhumane manner in which they have tried to strip this man of his livelihood for exercising his first amendment right. This kind of character assassination has been going on far too long. It is time for us to deal with it.

I believe we are fast approaching a crossroad in this country and we must make a serious decision as to which road we want to take. The people who have been ruling have placed us in a position of being despised by the world. We have few allies in the world any more. America is seen as a big bully that is fond of dropping bombs, creating chaos, destabilizing and capitalizing off of the destabilization. If we are to survive as a country and regain favor in the world, we have to make some drastic changes. The road we are on now will lead to certain destruction with more murder and depletion of the world's natural resources.

These decisions have to be made by the Africans in America who have always been, and still are, the spiritual backbone and moral compass of this country. President Barack Obama must be this change that he so skillfully campaigned on and won the presidency with. Business as usual, with warring on nations and usury on its own must cease. We must change. If we consciously and collectively decided to turn this country around, we could. If we collectively decided to be better, we could. If we hold the images of love, truth, peace, freedom and justice in our imagination long enough for these images to take shape, well, imagine that. If we collectively decide to love instead of hate and stop relying on anyone other than ourselves for instructions, we can save the planet. Until we have these discussions and make these decisions…God help us all…

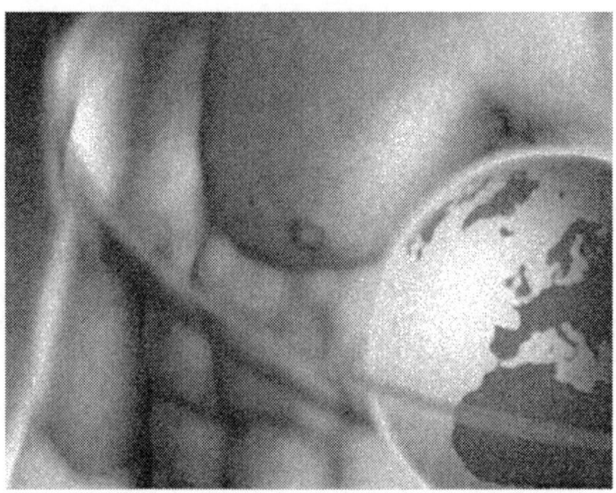

Original Illustrations and Graphics
by **JAXON** Visual Design & Illustration
http://jaxon.createaplace.com

Special Thanks to....

www.keepitR.E.A.L.productions.org
www.fellowshipofpraiseministries.org

CPSIA information can be obtained at www.ICGtesting.com
Printed in the USA
LVOW121821201112

308202LV00013B/27/P